Nichijo

Library of Congress Control Number 2014921614

ISBN-13: 978-0692326145

Nichijo:

The Testimony

of

John Provoo

As told to John Oliver

Nichijo

CONTENTS

The Author and the Hitchhiker

As the summer of 1983 began, I was making a living as a carpenter in the rural Puna district on Hawaii's Big Island. My son and I had a simple two-story house on the edge of volcanic rainforest that I bought half-built, and never did really finish. The world's most active volcano, the Pu'u O'o vent was about seven miles uphill on a gentle slope through the O'hia forest. It began erupting and continued almost once a month for years. When each outbreak occurred, we could walk up to the back road and see the glow from the fountain. It would shoot a red molten column 1500 feet straight into the air, making a huge hissing, whirring and rumbling sound; like massive machinery underground. Island people would hop in their cars and drive up to a vantage point.

We had three dogs. The smaller was the mother of the larger two, and the three bore no resemblance to each other. "Poi dogs" they're called. My old Ford pickup truck was a mongrel, too. It had been assembled from parts from about four different model years. A rear axle part broke as I was almost home one day so that I just barely coasted into my regular parking spot with the wheel and tire sticking out from the truck like a canoe's outrigger.

It wasn't a terribly difficult repair to undertake, except that getting the correct parts entailed walking and hitchhiking the 15 miles into Hilo where the Ford dealer could find them for me in the catalog. Returning the 15 miles to home, by the same walking and hitchhiking method I discovered that the truck was one year and the axle another year. I had to make drawings and take measurements and find model numbers and hitchhike down to the Ford dealer again to figure out what I needed. After much searching we found the parts I needed, except they didn't have them on this island, and ordered them shipped from Honolulu in five days.

It seemed there were about two weeks that it took me to fix this small problem and during that time, I hitchhiked everywhere, depending on the goodwill of a cross section of Island people.

Finally the day came when the truck was whole again and I drove it the three miles to the common rural mailboxes and turned left onto the paved two-lane "main road" that led down to Keaau. Less than a half-mile away at Makuu Drive was a tall Caucasian man in his sixties waiting calmly for a ride. He wore light blue Levi's, a lighter blue windbreaker, thong slippers and carried a kind of soft briefcase. I stopped to pick him up.

"I'm repaying a Karmic debt!" I said, as he got in and put his satchel on the seat between us. There was a whiff of incense as he opened it and shuffled around some papers, and some small black bound books inside. He gave me an odd look as I said it, but it was an odd comment. I explained that my own recent experience on the roadside on foot had made me grateful for the human willingness to give a stranger a lift.

It was obvious from the tools in the back of the truck that I did construction work and he began to ask me about that, and when I made a comment about enjoying the "Zen" of carpentry, about losing yourself in the act, he gave me another odd look.

"Do you know who I am? Do you know my history?" He asked. I said that I didn't. "I'm Nichijo. " He explained that he was a Buddhist priest, "A bishop, actually", and that he had a small group of priests and nuns studying with him in Hilo. I could see now that he wore the Ojuzu beads, the Buddhist rosary. He inquired what I knew about Buddhism.

I told him that I started learning about Buddhism in college and had incorporated what I understood into my own way of life.

About that time, we reached Keaau the intersection with the Hilo to Volcano highway, where I was stopping to visit my cohorts in the backroom of the local secondhand emporium. We found him a good spot to hitchhike, and saying that we hoped to talk again some day, said good-bye.

In the maze of old cane town buildings that adjoined Gaughen's Emporium, a few of the fellow carpenters that it was my great pleasure to work with were at their usual pastime of swapping gags and tales; and the store's owner, Tim Gaughen, was making comedy out of everything.

This day though, everyone had projects to attend to and errands waiting, and the gathering disbanded shortly after I got there. I was to continue on to Hilo to return a borrowed gear puller and left Tim talking on the phone.

As I climbed back in my truck I saw Nichijo still standing where I had left him, under the canopy of Akiyama store, out of the morning rain shower. I pulled up and he got back in. We continued down toward Hilo, another six miles away, and he asked about my college experience.

I described how at the University of California, Santa Barbara, I had spent seven years indulging my interests in Asia and oriental religions and examining my suspicions about the war in Vietnam. At the end of that time I received two bachelor's degrees, one in Religious Studies, and one in Political Science. I didn't care a thing about grades and scraped by with the minimum possible grade average to avoid the draft, receiving good marks only when the subject matter really excited me.

This was very interesting and relevant to him somehow. "I really must tell you about my legal problems, my struggles with the government."   By the time we reached Hilo he had outlined a yarn that as each mile rolled by, I became more convinced couldn't be true. It was too bizarre and preposterous. Yet the account had enough detail and coherence to it to allow me to suspend disbelief a while longer.

Our errands both ended up in the center of town, and his first stop was on my way, so I said would wait for him. He had me stop at the office of the Social Security Administration, near the corner of Kamehameha Boulevard and Volcano Highway. He invited me to come in with him. Inside the newish sort of modest two story storefront building, there was a long counter separating the office staff from the public. They seemed to know him.

"Reverend Shaka," said the friendly Japanese woman behind the counter, "what brings you here today?"

Nichijo was sifting through his papers and came up with the bundle he was looking for. It seemed that he was there on behalf of one of his parishioners. The person was to receive disability payments, which had been held up for one reason or another. There followed what could be described as a 15 minute theatrical performance that ranged from a hand wringing melodrama, to a rising crescendo of bluster and demands, softening to charm the clerk, rising again in uproar and outrage to invoke the names of this and that high bureaucrat on up to the Mayor and Governor, and the Bishops of the various hierarchies of Buddhist churches in Hawaii, then in quiet conspiratorial comic tones; "Couldn't she make some exception or waive some procedure or…?"

To my surprise, the bureaucratic barriers dissolved and disappeared; forms were filled out, applications were stamped, assurances were given that the check would be on its way to the needy applicant, everyone was thanked for their help and we were soon returning to the truck, mission accomplished.

His credibility had gone up in my mind and as we drove off I asked him some more about the details of his story, especially how as a prisoner of war, he had honed his skills of manipulating the system of his captors. I had just witnessed a minor demonstration in the SSA office. Except that no one was standing by with a saber to behead him if he blustered a little too far.

"Somebody ought to write a book about your story," I said, as we were pulling up in front of the hillside Hilo residence where some of his priests lived. "I *mean*," he said emphatically, rolling his eyes skyward.

It was probably three or four days later that I saw Nichijo again, this time he was looking for a ride in the other direction. We picked up his story where we had left off. It was out of my way, but I was intrigued again by the details of what I was being told and decided to take him past the turn off to my house, through Pahoa and up to his dojo, his temple. Past the center of this small town and up a rutted road of red volcanic cinder through the cane fields; then on to an unusually well paved section of one lane road, up into the rainforest. The property he called his dojo was at about the same elevation as my house, about five miles away through the nearly impenetrable jungle at the forest's floor.

There were barely two parking places off the road scraped of vegetation, with a base of chunky red cinder. We parked and I helped carry his packages the hundred or so feet along the slippery stone path. The forest is of the ubiquitous grey-green Ohia trees with their sometimes red, sometimes white, bottle brush flowers, towering giant hapuu ferns, and the popcorn of small vanda orchids poking up through the tangle of a small vining ferns which encroaches on every thing. In this forest, a building simply left unattended, and the area around it untrampled, will become engulfed and then swallowed by the vegetation in a few short months.

Calla lilies grew near the stairs to the dojo's front door. The stairs were literally falling apart, having become rotted from the continually wet conditions. The dojo itself was a one-room cabin with a flat roof and windows on three sides open to the outside. Nearly twenty cats of all descriptions clambered in and out of the building. He shouted out to them as he came up the path, "Babies! Kitties! Daaarlings! Daddy's home!" He had brought a medium sized bag of cat food and started immediately to dole out portions to all the cat dishes placed around the room so that each cat could eat within its own social and territorial comfort; some in groups, some alone. Each had a name and was a refugee some sort. He strategically separated problem combinations and resolved disputes between individuals.

The cats fed, watered and fussed over, he turned to his small shrine, lit some incense, bowed and chanted something in Japanese. Next he put a of pot water on the stove for tea. The single room had a kitchen sink, the stove and some ice chests used for food storage, a desk, several bookshelves crammed with books and papers, a closet area with some robes hanging, and a high bed platform with mosquito net draped over it.

It seemed that he would spend two or three nights a week there, on the average. It was mainly a place to house his cats and store his personal things. The rest of the time he would spend at an apartment in Hilo.

"I came into the possession of small fortunes several times in my life, and it always resulted in my losing myself and the fortune in a blur of alcoholism and debauchery. It was when events left me most impoverished, and my prospects most desperate, that I could appreciate the worth of the teaching. Compared to the conditions I've endured, this is a palace."

"When I asked the Lord Abbott at Minobu about my prospects for establishing a temple in Hawaii, he said, 'If you succeed you have failed, when you succeed, you will be old ashes, to be discarded.'"

"It's best to concentrate on the sutra, not the temple, because the conditions that brought my understanding into focus were not beautiful at all. They were the most outwardly horrible of locations and situations imaginable." As we drank our tea, he dug through his papers.

I decided to come back and replace the front stairs and I was beginning to take some notes, for somewhere along the way we had begun to talk of collaborating on his biography.

Hilo was a city of about 70,000 in those days and it had a very adequate public library. To its credit, the Hilo Library had The New York Times on microfilm. Searching the index, I looked up John David Provoo, the name Nichijo had been born with. There were 93 separate news articles. This was no made-up fable. My hitchhiking Buddhist friend was a genuine historical figure.

Over the next six months, I collected what clippings and materials I could, but it was slow going. Between doing my house building, being a Dad and having a life, I could only get down to the Hilo library once or twice a week for a few hours. I wasn't making substantial progress. I would have to take to the writing as a full time job: Get up in the morning and work at it all day, to get anything down on paper.

My twelve-year old son, JW, was planning to spend the following summer on the mainland with his grandparents, and my expenses would be minimal for those three months. My Mom agreed to make my land payments until the book was done. My ex-wife, Patti, who lived in Hilo, offered to take up the slack with whatever Johnny might need in the meantime, and do the typing of the final draft. A gateway had opened up, obstacles fell away and I began to occupy myself with my new mission full time.

These events started in June 1983 and most of our work took place in the summer of 1984. We had agreed to undertake the writing of his biography as a joint project. I would do what research I could and from time to time, interview him about what I had learned, write it up, read it to him for his correction and approval, and move on to another topic.

In the months that we labored on, I came to realize that he was indestructible in many ways and fragile in others. Collecting the early chapters was a breeze; an old priest's reminiscences of the path to his understanding, paying homage to his teachers and to the books that guided the way. He shared his adulation of the Buddha, his teachings, and all those in the brotherhood and sisterhood of Buddhism. Here's the world he set out to create for himself.

Working on subsequent chapters, we reconstructed the year of military service leading up to Pearl Harbor Day in Manila. He maintained a calm and detailed narrative. Then, the war began, and for the months he had witnessed increasing carnage at close hand. Reminded of all he had survived, and those he had seen butchered right before his eyes, some of our sessions were a renewed torment for him rather than any sort of catharsis. We were beginning to spelunk the darkest reaches of his memories. Some of our sessions were taking a toll on his state of mind.

Writing the years of prison camps was less traumatic, at least up until the end of the war. It was when he began to describe his Kafkaesque liberation, persecution and prosecution, that he displayed the extent to which betrayals had scarred him. In an innocent researcher's question, I mentioned the name one of the witnesses against him, as I had many times before. This time he became apoplectic and vented his rage at length. Following that session, I discovered that a few days later, he had checked himself in to the psychiatric ward at the Hilo Hospital, something he had apparently done many times over his years on the Big Island. The staff there knew him well and what to do, and in a week or so, he was his old self, and we went back to work.

By September, we had enough of a finished work to send off to the copyright office, and we began to seek a publisher. Copies were sent to all the obvious publishers, including one with whom Nichijo had mutual friend. That one was the most useful. I was a carpenter, a house builder. About the art of writing, I knew little. Except I knew that my first effort would likely be mediocre. I did have BA's in Political Science and Religious Studies, but that was the extent of my writing experience. The resulting manuscript had the tone of a lengthy undergraduate term paper. It was my hope that I find someone with a more sophisticated sense of good writing.

I began again with renewed enthusiasm, doing a re-write along the lines suggested by our contact in the publishing world. Things were proceeding as planned. Then one day, Nichijo came to our meeting apologetically saying that he couldn't go ahead with publication.

Some years earlier while Nichijo was still living on Oahu, reporters for the Honolulu Advertiser had gotten interested in his story. The articles written about him and the public response were quite distressing to him. It called into public attention his legal history and the old accusations. I think he began to realize that publishing the book would bring all that up once again, and he couldn't face it. I didn't have any choice except to honor his wishes and put the book, the rewrite and all my notes away in a box for another time. We copyrighted the latest version. And sent it off. I had to get back to making a living.

Years went by, and my son and I moved to California and finally to the San Francisco Bay Area where I live today. In the following years my contacts with Nichijo were fewer and my work on the re-write came to a halt. He died in August of 2001 and when I learned of his passing a few months later, I was on my way to China. I didn't get the chance to pay my respects at his gravesite until 2004. At the time of his death, all the prerogatives of our copyright became mine.

It has taken me a while to find the time to thoughtfully edit his words, so that he might finally have his story told in his own way. So, to honor a 30-year-old promise to an old friend, here is the testimony of John Provoo.

--- John Oliver   October 2014

Nichijo

Chapter One

Gold Fish in a Golden Pond

I would like to tell it all from the very beginning; exactly how it all unfolded; how step by step, and I came to be what I am, and how I came to be regarded as a traitor to my country. If just this once, my uninterrupted testimony is considered, it will be plain what happened to me. What will never be plain is why, and that I do not pretend to know.

I lived in a fairy tale. I felt like one of the large gold fish that nibbled on the mosses of the koi ponds; safe from predators, well fed, cared for. The koi pond in the Japanese Tea gardens in San Francisco's vast green Golden Gate Park was part of my playground. The park was an enormous maze of forest and meadows to explore and to act out my imaginary adventures. The destination of my quest would always be to reach this secret outpost of the far, far East: the sculpted and manicured paths, ornate orange pagodas, tiny bridges and ponds, the great gold and white Koi that swam there.

I was born John David Provoo, August 6, 1917, in San Francisco. When I was a kid, we lived in the Richmond district to the North of the park and I could easily make a bicycle tour from home East through the area known as "Japantown", back to the park to play in the Tea gardens, and make it home before lunch. I usually took much longer than that during the summer. I was drawn to the exotic feeling of the Japanese neighborhoods and markets and I would literally ride my bike up and down certain streets just to savor the kaleidoscope of cooking aromas.

The Tea Gardens had been created for the California Midwinter International Exposition of 1894. The man who had guided its building, Makoto Hagiwara, convinced the city leaders to maintain it as an attraction in the park after the fair closed. I got to know the Hagiwara family in the early 20's when I was in grade school. They lived in one of the traditional Japanese structures there and served as caretakers of the gardens. I became privileged to let myself in the back gate when the gardens were closed to the public. I would often come early in the morning, or at dusk. It was a quiet, calming realm for me. I needed that. I was an unusual kid.

Buddhism rang a bell for me at a very early age. The very first time I heard the chant of a Buddhist priest, though I could not translate a single word into English, I had the distinct feeling that I understood exactly what was being said.

The chant meant that there was another reality within the common one, obscured from awareness. Just as the words of what I was hearing were in my ears but not understood; a greater reality was all around us, within our ordinary perceptions, but unintelligible. I felt that the chant called out to learn the secrets.

San Francisco of the 1920's was a focal point of anti-oriental sentiment and racial tensions. The Caucasian-American majority feared the further influx of Asian immigrants: As coolie labor in the previous century, they had been tolerable, as farm labor or gardeners and fishermen they could be ignored and minimized. The succeeding generations had proven themselves all too capable of competing on an equal basis for jobs and commerce; and seemed increasingly successful in acquiring land and creating larger scale agriculture.

This was the era of the Alien Land Law in California, 1924, legislation declaring that persons of Asian descent could only own land under certain circumstances. The Supreme Court upheld that persons of Japanese descent could not be naturalized, and that any U.S. citizen who married a Japanese would lose his or her citizenship.

In San Francisco there were many little "Japantown" neighborhoods, where Orientals lived in their peculiar ways, ate rice, raw fish, octopus and seaweed. A scornful common term for them was "Buddhaheads". At that time, the Christian majority in this country regarded Buddhism as a relic of pagan idol-worship and would ultimately become extinct as Christianity replaced heathen beliefs in all the dark corners of the globe. Buddhist churches were few in these days, and many "temples" were merely homemade shrines in a corner of a Japanese home or business. Caucasian Buddhists were extremely rare, and I, a Caucasian child following his own inspiration, was the unlikeliest Buddhist of all. I have to say, it never bothered me to be different, in fact, I reveled in it. If we were all in an ice cream shop and everyone was ordering Vanilla, I would have to have tutti-frutti.

My brother George tells the tale of me rescuing ants from drowning in the kitchen sink. I remember doing things like that a lot. I even took a serious fall and cracked my skull when I was six, trying to rescue a cat on our balcony. I have always been highly sensitive to the plight and suffering of any living being.

I was seven in 1924, and as children are, had been oblivious to the prejudices of the adults. As I was growing up, it became increasingly clear that the society around me didn't share my love of things Japanese. In fact, there was more and more hostility toward them and toward me, I was so often in their company. Most of my friends were Japanese.

In 1926, my family moved twenty miles south to Burlingame. I couldn't visit the park as often and made efforts to recreate the experience. I made a shrine in my room, and bought little Buddha incense burners at Woolworth's. I clipped from the pages of National Geographic whatever pictures of Buddhist statues and temples I could find, and displayed them on my altar. I would stand before this array, light incense, bow and chant my made-up chants.

My father thought this behavior to be an obsession that would lead nowhere. He tried to derail or at least sidetrack and once even burned some of my books. My mother was able to convince him to let my interests run their course. "The boy will grow out of it."

Well, of course, the boy didn't grow out of it. I continued to read everything I could find about the subject. I read the life of Buddha. I read of a young a prince in Northern India who abandoned his advantages in order to explore his own mind and to understand sickness, suffering, old age and death. I collected information about monasteries and monks, and began to add more authenticity to my chants, stringing together the different names and titles of the Buddha into an exotic-sounding litany.

One day when I was eleven, I used scissors to cut off all my hair, as short as I could, wrapped myself in an orange bedspread, and with a small bowl, walked into the hills. I was trying it on, play-acting how it was to be the young prince embarking upon a spiritual path. I sat down beneath an oak tree to meditate. By dinnertime I returned. A little too young to depart for Asia, but that was my childhood dream. The path would be ready for me, when I was ready for it.

We had a large basement in our house in Burlingame, and a more traditional form of play-acting was being nurtured. We were a literate, theatrical family at home. We four brothers, Frank, Myself, George and Robert, were encouraged to follow intellectual and artistic pursuits. We had an extensive library of the classics of Western literature, encyclopedias, atlases, the works of western philosophers and the poetry and reflections of Whitman, Emerson and Thoreau. My eldest brother, Frank, had a definite inspiration for dramatic acting and directing, and would write short plays and skits for the entertainment of family and friends. We would present them in our basement theater. I was the second son, and I was always eager to take part in these events. Any school play that came along, I was in it. I loved the costumes, the putting on of another identity; I was good at that.

It was while I was in the sixth grade at Roosevelt Grammar School that I first saw the inside of an actual Buddhist Temple. It was part of a Japanese laundry building in San Mateo. It was a very small one but it had an exquisite black lacquered altar cabinet with a standing figure of the Buddha inside. I had come to the laundry with a Japanese friend and there was no service going on at the time. When I discovered that there was a Sunday school service held there for the few Japanese children in the area, I joined.

In the next few years, my interest deepened and I was acquiring a large library of Buddhist books. Once a month, a priest would come down from San Francisco to perform the service. This was the time when I first heard the priest chanting and had the distinct feeling that I understood, and an inescapable feeling that the message was for me, personally.

By the time I had reached my first year in high school, I realized that my curiosity had become so serious, that my path had to include studying in Asia. The realization both thrilled me and forebode the homesickness I knew I would feel. This would be the central conflict of my adolescence and all the events of my life pointed toward a day when I would be prepared intellectually, emotionally and spiritually to go; when either I had my parent's permission or was old enough to go regardless; and of course, when I had the money to pay my way. That day was to be ten more years in coming.

Our family moved back to San Francisco, and for a few semesters, I attended Commerce High School. My interests led me to explore the established Buddhist temples in the city. They were, of course, located in the Chinatown and Japantown districts and there were quite a number of them.

My interests led me of course to have extensive contacts with Japanese people and it was becoming increasingly apparent that the society around me was racially prejudiced in the extreme. It was something that I wanted to ignore; I hoped that it would pass away. I would find myself the object of hateful glares when seen in the company of kimono-clad

Japanese girls. Events like these darkly contrasted with the idealistic "bridges of understanding" that were the theme of so many of my Buddhist books. East was meeting west, but in a horrible way.

One of my friends at Commerce High School was Robert Yamanaka, who also attended the same temple. Robert was Japan born, and before the war he would return to Japan. Few realize that for some, the war was like our American civil war, or probably many wars, had elements of brother against brother, friend vs. friend. Years later, Robert and I came face to face in that horrible war in the Pacific. He had become a Japanese soldier.

My brother, Frank, had been offered several drama scholarships and had accepted one from the Pasadena Community Playhouse in Southern California, and my visits with him gave me opportunities to experience Buddhist temples in all parts of the state.

I learned about the Triple Jewel: The Buddha, the Dharma (the Teachings) and the Sangha (the Community). You do not find enlightenment on your own. I had realized that I needed to find genuine instruction in order to progress. I finally met Bishop Masuyama Kenju at the Hongwanji temple in San Francisco and under him took the next step to become formally accepted as a novice priest. The vows taken upon becoming a novice define tasks that are infinite, not to be completed in a lifetime. The Bodhisattva Vow:

Innumerable are all sentient beings; I vow to save them all.

Inexhaustible are human passions and ignorance; I vow to overcome them all.

84,000 in number are the gates of the True Law; I vow to learn them all.

Most difficult is the path sublime, which leads to complete enlightenment,

I vow to attain it.

Bishop Maysuyama Kenju was head of the Jodo Shinshu sect, numerically the largest in Japan. As always, I was an eager student and quickly learned the teachings of the Pure Land and Tendai schools and the differences between the various schools of Buddhism throughout the world. The differences are, basically, their choice of the Buddha's discourses, or sutras, which they emphasize.

On the occasion of a very high Abbot of the Shin sect's visit to the United States, I was elevated to full priest. The abbot was Prince Otani, a direct descendant of Saint Shinran, the founder. He was on his way to Washington, D.C. to make a call on the president and made a stop in San Francisco. The young novices who were studying under Bishop Masuyama were presented to him as candidates and Prince Otani himself administered the vows of the Sangha, the brotherhood of priests:

"Do you understand upon entering the Sangha, that:

For abiding place, you may have only a tree or a cave?

For clothing you may have only rags?

For food, you may have only what is left over from others,

 Or what is clean and freely given?

 For medicine you may have only urine?"

    While these vows were meant as a willingness to seek a humble path and forego the pursuit of worldly comforts, for me, they were especially prophetic. That wasn't the half of it.

    In the meantime, my brother, Frank had returned from Southern California and made a big success as a radio actor at KFRC in San Francisco. He had been so successful in his acting and creating of new programs that he was hired by NBC to go to New York to continue his career, and created such early radio dramas as <u>My Son and I</u> for the <u>Kate Smith Hour</u> and <u>Concerning Miss Marlowe</u>. He wrote and acted for <u>Texaco Star Theater</u> and many others and much later, television shows like <u>From These Roots</u>.

    Through my brother's reputation, I was given an audition at KFRC. I did very well apparently, and had no trouble performing, owing to my experience in our basement theater in Burlingame. My first roles were juvenile, but soon I proved myself capable of a whole range of voices. The radio work was exciting and paid very well, but the rehearsal and broadcast schedules conflicted with regular school attendance, so I transferred to night school.

This was 1933 and 1934, at the end of alcohol prohibition, a time when a speakeasy in San Francisco was easier to find than a water fountain. I floated into my brother's high life of big paychecks, flashy cars, smoke-filled studios and highballs for lunch, with ease. I did my parts at KFRC, learned that I had affinity for debauchery, scattered the money like flower petals, spent too much time in those nightclubs.

I continued with my Buddhist studies but two parts of my nature were developing, at odds with each other. Just when I had taken vows accepting poverty, I had been steered into San Francisco's fast lane. I was the sincere, searching, scholarly mystic ...a Buddhist Priest; and I was the flamboyant and theatrical prodigy of materialistic America. I was becoming a man with two heads, irreconcilable heads.

I began to correspond actively with Buddhist scholars in all parts of the world, including such notables as D.T. Suzuki, Christmas Humphries and the great Indian poet, Rabindranath Tagore. I also had a great deal of correspondence with Reverend Earnest Shinkaku Hunt, an Englishman who had become a Buddhist priest and settled in Hawaii, and met him in person during several summer vacation trips in the islands. I had extensive correspondence with a Dutch Buddhist in Java named Van Dienst, who invited me to live and study at the temple there.

My horizons were expanding. I explained to Bishop Masuyama that I wished to go to Japan and pursue further studies in the Shin school of which the Bishop was a part. The Bishop explained that his position in the Shinshu was a hereditary one and that in his own mind he felt that I was beyond that teaching already and that I was ready for the Lotus

Sutra, the highest teaching, which the Buddha had taught during the last eight years of his life.

During this period, I met Edward Fricke, a wealthy San Francisco socialite, at Temple, and had been asked up to his California Street Mansion to read Buddhist books for him. Fricke was virtually blind and had great difficulty reading for himself. At the end of their first reading he offered me a $100 bill. I refused the money and told him that I was happy to read for him. This began a long association in which I was introduced into the upper strata of San Francisco society, names that will mean little to you now; the Templeton-Crocker's, Frederick Julius McNear, George Kleiser, Jr., Count DeClauson, Lady Rose, Baroness Von Rautcuf, Baroness Von Pistolacurst, and members of the Catholic hierarchy, notably Father Gleason, the top Jesuit in California and Father Gregory DeWitt, an Augustine from Belgium, who was an extremely gifted artist and was allowed to travel with his collection. Anyway, it was a rarified atmosphere.

Accompanying Edward Fricke to St. Mary's each Sunday for Mass, I became acquainted with Noel Sullivan, who had given his inherited $17,000,000 dollar estate at Carmel to the Catholic Church in order to renounce the world and enter a Jesuit monastery. For a seeker of a higher plane, this confluence of wealth and voluntary poverty was dazzling.

My radio career was expanding also and I took jobs with other radio stations, took all sorts of speaking parts, paid political announcements of Socialist candidates that others were unwilling to do, and interviewed some of the top athletes of the day: Max Baer, Baron Von Kram and others. And all this when I was just sixteen and seventeen. And I had a very good time but I was too easily lured by the booze and fast life that was available to me at this tender age.

Now I was the young prince who had it all. I had become so successful in the material realm that now it would be meaningful to renounce it; and important to do so, I thought, before I became hopelessly addicted to that life. I opted for the ascetic pursuit of the Buddhist Priesthood. I hoped it would cure my two-headedness.

So in 1935, I went to work as a lowly clerk in the Federal Reserve Bank in San Francisco, a job I kept for five years, making less than a tenth of what I had been making at the radio stations and diligently saving for my passage to Japan, at first swimming with difficulty against the currents of temptation. The stoic stone columned Federal Reserve Bank building on Sansome Street was my refuge. Its gates and locks and timetables, and need for steady precision that the world of numbers requires, kept me from drifting back.

Naturally, I become involved with the growing number of Caucasian Buddhists that seemed to gravitate toward Bishop Masuyama's Hongwanji temple. Some were a bohemian fringe, with earnest but sometimes zany expressions of their pursuit. I would find them with the shades down all day in incense filled rooms, wearing lots of meditation beads, hypnotically chanting and endlessly discussing Eastern texts. At the same time they had serious interests in the English transmission of Buddhist literature and undertook many successful projects; films, art exhibits and lectures organized under the auspices of the English Department at the Hongwanji Temple. The head of the department was an American named Robert Stewart Clifton, who had been ordained a missionary priest in Japan.

He started a magazine they called The Middle Path, which later became The American Buddhist.

For a short time, I took up the study of Zen under the great Zen Master, Nyogen Senzaki, mentor to the "Beat" generation a decade later, but then I became aware of the Lotus Sutra.

Sometime in 1936, I received a copy of the latest translation into English of the Lotus Sutra, by H. Kerns. It came as a complete revelation to me. It was one of those experiences in which someone else had verbalized my innermost thoughts and put them into print. There are hundreds of schools of Buddhist teaching, each one emphasizing a certain sutra in a certain way. When I discovered my own innate concurrence with the Lotus Sutra, it became clear that I should focus my studies through the Nichiren School, which is based in Japan and formulated almost entirely around the Lotus teaching. The Lotus Sutra is the final teaching of the historic Buddha, transmitted to a multitude of followers on Vulture Peak. It proclaims the Buddha to be the embodiment of eternal enlightenment; the realization that this is the perfect world: and that Nirvana and the everyday world are one in the same. The Nichiren School was established to reaffirm this as the ultimate doctrine.

"Namu myoho-renge-kyo", literally, "Adoration to the Lotus Sutra."

Or, as I say after my years sculpting my understanding of this sutra, I 've come to think of it this way:

"Adoration to the Lotus Sutra,

Adoration to the mysterious perfection of everything, just as it is."

That chant, with that meaning, is as deeply ingrained in me as breathing, and it has been a vision that comforted me through years of the most terrifying events in the most horrible circumstances.

I began searching for an English-speaking priest of that school in San Francisco and hopefully, a mission. I found a branch of the orthodox school of Nichiren in the person of Bishop Ishida Nitten.

Bishop Ishida had his temple in a large converted residence, with a large shrine downstairs and living quarters upstairs and in the back. In the attic of the house lived the American sculptress Gertrude Boyle Kanno, whose husband was Japanese. They had had difficulty in finding a place to rent, as they were a "mixed race" couple. The racism, particularly in regard to Japanese in San Francisco was difficult to avoid in these times, and it was creating a disturbing conflict in me.

Bishop Ishida spoke very little English, and in the style typical of teacher-student relations in the East, he would put me off, saying, "Go away," or "I am much too busy," or "Come back another time." A prospective disciple is tested and prepared in this way. I kept going back. Finally the Bishop gave me a collection of letters that he had laboriously translated from the Chinese into English. I had been accepted and instruction had begun, but slowly.

A traditional saying in the East is "when the disciple is ready, the master will appear." I came across another smaller temple in a two-story house with the garage underneath made into an orthodox Nichiren temple. The priest was a cheerful round-faced man with glasses named Aoiyagi Shoho, who later became Bishop Nippo. He was from a priestly family whose ancestral home is at Ichinose, not far from one of the major temples of the Nichiren sect. This time my reception was entirely different. On my first visit the priest welcomed me warmly. "Please come, come in," which was practically the extent of his English. It was a relationship that seemed to be fully developed at the first meeting, although neither of us could speak the other's language, and the relationship would last with the same strength for our lifetimes. We taught each other our respective languages, and night after night we studied the Lotus Sutra, often until after midnight. My understanding of this highest teaching was intertwined with the learning of the Japanese language and most of the realizations came to me without first being translated into English ...I had quickly reached the stage where I could think in Japanese ...I could think and express my deepest thoughts in Japanese. At times I felt that East and West were unified within me, but in the external world events were pulling East and West apart. The Lotus seemed the only thing that resolved all contradictions. I memorized the 16th chapter in Japanese, and often chanted it from that day forward. In it, Buddha says to his audience:

Beneath the dark surface of this crumbling illusion,

My perfect world shimmers with light.

Though this illusion seems burning,

And these suffering beings lie broken and bleeding,

My perfect world is here,

And these beings are whole and filled with light.

I have revealed the fate of the world:

That all beings shall be illumined."

During these years at the bank and studying under Reverend Aoiyagi, I had been saving toward the expense of traveling to the Far East and experiencing a great deal of conflict about going at all. My mother, who was my confidant in most things, favored my going through with it. My father was against it and would not have allowed me to go. I had to wait at least until the age of legal majority. My master, Reverend Aoiyagi, of course, encouraged me to go, but my girlfriend saw it as the likely end, for us. The debate of course was mostly going on within me, it was two worlds struggling to claim me and I was not certain that I would survive the contest: I might be torn apart. At one point, on the advice of members of my family, I sought the opinion of an alienist, which was the term for psychiatrist in those days, Dr. Joseph C. Catton. After listening to my conflict, Dr. Catton advised me to go through with my plan. "You may be disillusioned if you go, but if you don't, you'll remember it all your life, and regret not having done so." It was sound advice on the face of it, and I took it to heart.

Finally, the course of romance made up my mind. My girlfriend went to Indiana to attend college for a semester. We wrote every week and when she returned to San Francisco on vacation, I asked her to marry me before returning for the following semester. When she left for Indiana that year, I felt that my last distraction departed with her. I would focus on the

Buddhism.

Reverend Aoiyagi had written to the temple authorities in Japan, telling them of my conversion and desire to enter the monastery there. It was Reverend Aoiyagi's wish to accompany me, in order to introduce me, sponsor me and facilitate my entry into formal training. I gave notice at the bank and paid my fare on the NYR line to Yokohama, Japan.

In March of 1940, the day of my embarkation arrived, several robed priests came to my house, a temporary altar was erected in my living room, and incense and prayers were offered. The entourage left in a caravan of automobiles, stopping at several temples on the way. When we arrived at dockside, several hundred well wishers, many of them Japanese, were there to see Reverend Aoiyagi and myself off.

Resplendent in my full robes, I stood with my parents saying goodbye. At the last moment my mother and father switched roles. My mother had always been my patroness and it was my father who characteristically said, "Well, the jay-birds will have to feed him." Now it was my mother who said "Oh Daddy, Daddy, don't let him go." My father turned to her and said, "Why, he'll make the finest damn 'Budda' priest there ever was."

Nichijo

Chapter Two

Butterfly and Tiger

My family and friends stood on the dock; I stood high above at the ship's railing in my robes. Enormous ropes were the last things that tethered us to the continent. Gangplanks were hoisted up, the lines were cast off and the great ship pulled away. The throng faded, the dock faded, the city faded and finally the brand new Golden Gate Bridge, painted tori-gate orange, faded from view. As the ship churned its way west into the setting sun and darkening Pacific Ocean, I felt as though I were casting off on a great symbolic ocean: a young prince on a mystic quest, a modern Siddhartha leaving the palace. I wasn't looking back. I felt a great sense of mission. The English translations of Buddhist writings that had been the mainstay of my intellectual development contained the pervasive theme of creating a "bridge of understanding between East and West". That's what I wanted my life to be. And all the efforts of my life would be spent in that creation. My sense of mission deepened in the weeks at sea.

Our destination was the temple complex at Minobu, where Nichiren, the founder, had spent the last eight years of his life. Nichiren was both a historical and legendary figure. His name means "Sun-Lotus". He was born in the fishing village of Rominato; the southeastern-most point in Japan where, it is said, the rising sun first touches the shores of the nation.

Legend has it that at his conception, Nichiren's mother dreamed of a tiny sun coming to rest on a lotus blossom. On the day of his birth, a spring of clear water gushed forth in the corner of their garden and hundreds of white lotuses had blossomed in the cold waters of the bay... signaling the birth of a great man.

He was born in 1222, during a feudal period in Japanese history in which the country was ruled by a succession of shoguns, military dictators who rose to power through inter clan warfare and ruled from the capital at Kamakura.

He had an early interest in Buddhism and entered the monastery near his home at age eleven. From his earliest days, he was disturbed by his country's perpetual internal warfare and the fragmentary proliferation of innumerable Buddhist sects their rivalries even becoming murderous at times. He became conscious of the chasm between the peasants and the wealthy; the poverty and malnutrition of the masses and the indifference of their masters. He couldn't understand how it was that Buddhism, which was supposed to bring harmony and peace, had failed so miserably; and why the lofty priesthood ministered carefully to the aristocracy and ignored the plight of the masses. He concluded that most of the sects must have been teaching false doctrines.

The singular quest of his youth, then, was to discover the true form and the true teaching of Buddhism. He traveled all over Japan and studied at all of the great temples of all the sects and by the age of thirty-one he had determined that the Lotus Sutra was the ultimate word of the Buddha and that the unification of the country could only be achieved by using the Lotus as the basis of governing.

Returning to the small temple near his home where he had begun, he preached his first sermon. He exalted the Lotus and denounced all other teachings as false and destructive. When the ruling lord of Kominato heard of this he was outraged and ordered Nichiren's execution, but he had already left the district.

For the next seven years, he traveled the outer provinces and delivered his teachings, gaining important disciples and allies among the scattered warlords, and formulating his plan for saving the nation, predicting the Mongol invasions, which came true in 1274.

In 1260, he completed his Rissho Ankoku Ron, a discourse on the country's ailments and a procedure for restoring it. He presented it to an officer of the military government in Kamakura, but received no response. He began to speak his mind before the impoverished crowds in the streets of the city. He was becoming too revolutionary to be tolerated.

The ruling family and members of the officially sanctioned Nembutsu priesthood incited a mob to burn his hermitage and kill him, but, according to legend, a white monkey awakened him and led him to safety. Again he fled to the outer provinces.

The following year he had returned to Kamakura and to his outspoken ways, and this time he was charged with disturbing the peace and exiled to the Izu Peninsula, a common sentence for political agitators. The intention was to silence him for good. Instead of leaving him on the shore they stranded him on a rocky islet at low tide. The rock – Mana Ita, would be completely covered when the tide came in, and he would be swept away. Instead, he was rescued by an old fisherman and subsisted on Izu for nearly two years. He was able to gain pardon by curing the local lord on Izu of his madness.

The very next year, he returned to his birthplace because his mother lay dying and he was said to have brought her back from death. When he heard that Nichiren was in the district, Lord Kagenobu of Kominato, who had ordered him executed eleven years before, organized an ambush. A number of Nichiren's entourage were killed by arrows and swords and as Lord Kagenobu himself charged Nichiren with his sword raised, Nichiren calmly stood his ground, holding his *ojuzu*, his prayer beads. A flash of sunlight from the beads startled the horse, Lord Kagenobu was thrown and struck his head on a rock, and Nichiren was saved.

In 1268 one of Nichiren's prophesies from the Rissho Ankoku Ron concerning the invasion of foreign armies appeared to be about to come true, and Nichiren stepped up his campaign. Kubli Kahn, the Mongol emperor of China, was demanding tribute and threatening invasion. This time Nichiren's efforts earned him a charge of treason and though he was officially sentenced to banishment, an execution had been secretly planned.

The night he was to be sent into exile, he was instead taken to a place of execution and he calmly prepared himself for his end. As he kneeled on a straw mat, the executioner raised his sword and a ball of light is said to have appeared in the sky. The swordsman became dizzy and dropped his sword to the ground.

Instead of being killed, Nichiren was sent into exile on Sado Island, off the Northwest coast of Japan's main island, Honshu. He remained on Sado three years when the military ruler at Kamakura, fearing the impending Mongol invasion, pardoned him and had him returned to the capital. The Shogun asked for Nichiren's advice. Nichiren insisted that the government turn away from all other sects of Buddhism and take refuge in the Lotus. The Shogun refused.

Nichiren left Kamakura and moved to the western side of Mt. Fuji, to the slopes of Mt. Minobu; he built a small hermitage where he intended to live in seclusion, though hundreds would come to hear him teach. His health was poor from years of malnutrition in exile and he wished to live out his days at Minobu. He spent the last eight years of his life there, teaching and writing. He was on his way to the hot springs at Ikegami when he died. His ashes are enshrined at Minobu.

As I was arriving in Japan nearly 700 years later, I wasn't anticipating an experience that included official persecution, exile, near execution and charges of treason. These were more peaceful, civilized times, and the Nichiren School, Nichirenshuj, was well established.

Our arrival as young priest and master in Yokohama was on one of those rare days when Mt. Fuji is visible. The lower slopes were covered with clouds, and the ancient volcano shone brightly above giving it the appearance of floating in the air. There was a reception for Reverend Aoiyagi and me at the hotel in Yokohama where we spent the first night. The following day we made the 100-mile train ride to the beautiful valley on the far side of Mt. Fuji.

We arrived in the town of Minobu in the late afternoon and found a room in the Tamaya Inn. In the morning we arose long before dawn to climb Mt. Minobu to the temple to arrive in time for the morning otsutome, the worship service conducted each day in the founder's hall.

Garbed in white robes, we started up the mountain through the great sammon, a mammoth gateway and up the Bodhisattva stairs, a huge oversized stone stairway. The stairway led up to a large plateau, some 300 feet long. As we reached the top of the stairs, we could see the giant facade of the Kuonji, the founder's hall: a centuries old temple with vast eaves extending over the verandas. It was breathtaking. To me it was stepping six or seven hundred years into the past. It had indeed remained unchanged for that length of time in its appearance and function. The monastery and temple complex is set in a great quiet misty grove of cryptomeria trees. Their appearance is much like large redwood trees, except their branches look like cloud formations. At Minobusan there is often a mist the Japanese call kiri that gives an ethereal appearance to everything, completing the atmosphere of reverence and other-worldliness.

We entered the temple. To the measured beat of the drum, all the pilgrims were chanting the odaimoku, "Namu Myoho-renge-kyo" as they waited for the Lord Abbot, his entourage, and all the other priests, monks and novices to enter and start the morning service. It was dark and a priest mounted the stairway and struck flint in the center and both sides of the central part of the shrine, where two vast doors remained closed. He then lit two candles and the two doors were slowly opened to reveal the seated figure of St. Nichiren, the founder. The drumbeat reached a crescendo and then stopped. The ancient bugakyu music began as the Lord Abbot entered from behind the shrine and prostrated himself before the high altar three times, then proceeded to the back of the temple where he climbed a stairway to a high throne-like pile of cushions, with a small gong at his right hand and at his left hand a book of the dead, containing the names and the death dates of those persons and patriarchs to be remembered this particular morning.

Mochizuki Nichiken, the Lord Abbot, chanted several invocations and then named the chapter of the sutra to be read that morning. Simultaneously, the several rows of monks lifted the wooden covers off their eight volumes of the Lotus Sutra in red boxes and all turned to the indicated chapter.

During the course of the service, I was led to a raised dais, close to the shrine, surrounded with a low lacquer fence, and at the appropriate time was told that I could offer incense. After bowing to the Lord Abbot, I turned to the shrine and offered incense three times, in reverence to the Buddha, the Dharma and the Sangha; triple jewel of the Lotus, and then returned to the dais where I had been and sat down on the cushion.

Later that same morning, after we had breakfasted in the monastery I was coached for my presentation to the Abbot. I was then taken to a huge reception hall. At the far end of the hall the Lord Abbot was seated on a raised dais. I was required to make several bows as I proceeded down this long massive hall toward him. I felt as though I were growing smaller and smaller as I approached and the Abbot loomed larger and more formidable. Finally I reached the dais and made my last bow and looked up. The Abbot said to me, in Japanese, "It is well you have come. You are my disciple. Now get out." It was not until that moment that I knew that I would be accepted. It was a great honor to be accepted as a novitiate by a master who was over thousands of monks and priests.

There was a sadness about this as well, because I was deeply attached to Reverend Aoiyagi. He would soon return to his parish and duties in San Francisco. There was time for us to share a few days exploring the temple complex and the sylvan mountainside of Minobu. We climbed the mountains behind the main temple. We were going to a small temple very high up the slopes of Mt. Minobu.

I had gone on some distance ahead, since my legs were much longer then Aoiyagi's and reached the temple a few minutes before him. The priestess of the temple bowed as I approached but as soon as she could see me closely, her eyes grew large, and her expressionless face could not mask her anxiety. I bowed and greeted her in Japanese. As she made tea and prepared oranges for her guest, she did not turn her back or take her eyes off of me for one second.

Soon Aoiyagi approached the temple and the priestess looked anxiously back and forth as between he and I as we conversed in English. When Aoiyagi explained to the woman that I was a priest from America, she asked, "What's that?" Aoiyagi replied that America was a land far across the ocean, and she said, "But his eyes ...they're blue" Aoiyagi explained that there were many in America that looked like me. Only then did the priestess relax. She said that when I first walked up, she had thought that I was the fox-god. I was the first Caucasian she had ever seen. Imagine, she thought she was in the presence of the fox god, and she served him tea and oranges.

Soon Aoiyagi left to return to San Francisco, and I began my formal training. For the first few weeks, I was quartered in a monastery dormitory with other novices. Then, a single dwelling was made available for me that was close to the Lord Abbot's villa, the Minobusan college building, and the various temples. It was agreed that I would undertake to teach English to the novice students attending the College.

The world at Minobusan was everything I had hoped it would be. It was the ancient and classical Buddhist training in every sense. It was completely separated from the outside world. It was harmonious, it was beautiful, it was immaculately clean, it was calm; it was so well run that I always knew exactly where I should be at any given moment and what my duties were. There was time for study, there was time for meditation, there was time for work, there was time for ceremony, time for eating, time for bathing and even time, if I stayed up late enough, to write letters home.

The diet provided to novice monks was by design minimal as a part of their often-harsh training. It was barely adequate for the typical Japanese novice, but for my somewhat larger occidental frame it represented malnutrition. As a rare Caucasian, my training was made extra harsh; I was not expected to complete the rigors of the novices' monastic experience. I was given the daily job of cleaning the toilets for nearly a year. I became thin and frail, and when finally it became apparent that I would persevere even though I was literally wasting away, I was allowed to go to the Tamaya Inn in Minobu Village once a week to eat meat.

In the home of one of my socialite sponsors in San Francisco hung a magnificent scroll painting of a butterfly reflected in a pond. A tiger lurks nearby, tensing itself to pounce: That's me at Minobu, 1941. The butterfly is an image of self-admiring serenity, the tiger a harsh reality about to turn quiet into chaos. In just this way, the blissful experience I was enjoying at Minobusan would not last. Beyond the confines of the monastery, menacing forces were gathering in anticipation of an unprecedented cataclysm. Except two tigers were circling each other, and I, the butterfly, was of no interest to them.

My English teaching duties were expanded to include teaching students in the local middle school. I became aware that there was an acute food shortage. Many of my students had a sickly greenish appearance and I learned that many of them had resorted to catching and eating salamanders on their way to school to supplement their diets.

At the end of six months training, I began to be allowed to go on excursions, always robed and in the company of other monks and priests, to visit various shrines and temples. When on these excursions to Nara, Nikko, Tokyo-Yokohama and Kamakura, I became keenly aware of a general state of suppressed excitement, of hostility just below the surface. Posters in the train stations cautioned the public not to speak to foreigners. The posters depicted a grotesque Uncle Sam, some with a great big ear.

I began to come under the scrutiny of the civilian authorities, first at the local police station in Minobu. I was required to make a lengthy statement as to my intentions and the duration of my stay. On my few brief travels, I was approached by police and questioned, though the robes of a prestigious Buddhist Order insulated me from direct harassment.

I received a communication from the American Embassy in Tokyo that I should make an appearance there, which I did. It was suggested that I return to the United States. I replied that I didn't wish to do so, that I was in the country for the purpose of training for the priesthood, that I hadn't completed my training and that I intended to return to the United States after my ordination.

Japan was at war on the Asian continent, at the time, in Manchuria and China. The Dutch, the British and the Americans were ratcheting up their economic sanctions, and everyday people were feeling the effects. Japan was a country with few natural resources other than timber and coal. Its heavy industries were being stagnated by the shortage of oil and scrap metal, which previously had been imported in large quantities. There was a severe economic depression in the country and it was not uncommon for someone to faint in the street from malnutrition. There was increasing bitterness among the population that was being amplified and encouraged by the press. On several occasions I was asked, "Why is it that President Roosevelt wants to make war against us?"

War was spoken of everywhere by the Japanese population. My excursions would take me past schoolyards where grade school children drilled with wooden rifles. I witnessed the return of shiploads of the ashes of their fallen soldiers, and many patriotic rallies. At the hot springs at

Shimobe, I would see many, many wounded soldiers there taking their soaks in the numerous hot baths. Their open wounds didn't seem to disconcert them in the slightest. They were tough and battle-hardened. On the streets, everywhere, there were uniforms. The military party in Japanese politics was becoming increasingly dominant. The military forces on the Asian mainland seemed at times to act as completely independent entity, out of the control of the headquarters in Japan. I felt a great concern about the direction of events: Relations between Japan and the United States were running exactly opposite what I had hoped. The bridge between East and West was starting to burn, and I had to choose which shore.

I received more communications from the American embassy, each successively couched in a little firmer language, a little more direct. I was called in for a number of interviews and at one point was told, "Well, we will call your passport" or, "We will require you to make another passport." And each time I replied, "If that's what's necessary, that's what I will do."

The Japanese authorities were taking note of my repeated visits to the embassy, and finally I was taken to police headquarters in Tokyo and questioned exhaustively. There was a growing dossier on John Provoo in the files of both the Japanese and American authorities, the beginnings of a web of suspicions that would entangle me for the rest of my life.

When I would return from these visits to Minobu, I would find in that placid atmosphere only compassion, wisdom, understanding and peace, but I remained disturbed about what was transpiring outside. I had become close to the Lord Abbot in my stay there. He and everyone became aware of my predicament. I was urged to stay, in fact, an official of the prefecture in which the monastery was located told me that in the event of war with the U.S., I would be guaranteed immunity from incarceration and harassment.

At one interview at the American Embassy, I was told that if I didn't return to the United States very soon, it was likely that I would not be able to do so for many years, if at all, in which case I would probably never see my parents alive again. As it turned out this would have been the case since my mother died before I returned from my wartime experience. On the other hand, the Lord Abbot was getting very old and it was likely that if I did leave I would never see my master alive again. The embassy personnel were understandably circumspect about their reasons for pressuring me to return. They would not say directly that war was coming, and finally I asked to see the ambassador himself, Joseph C. Grew.

The ambassador was refreshingly understanding of my situation. He himself was a great student of Japanese culture and an expert calligraphist. He was highly respected by the Japanese people and was placed under protective guard after the outbreak of war and eventually exchanged through Lorenzo Marques, capitol of the neutral Portuguese territory, Mozambique.

I was receiving two sorts of letters from the United States; my mother was advising me to stay and complete my training; Antoinette, my friend from the Reserve Bank, and I had been corresponding since I had came to Minobu. She had been supportive of my spiritual quest, but now she was beginning to sense the peril of my presence there.

My dream of monastic utopia and the unification of my

own psyche had become a new fitful conflict. I saw it as two distinct choices: To remain in Japan, continue my studies for the priesthood and dedicate my life to peace and enlightenment; or, to return to America, abandon Buddhist training and probably be drafted into the Army.

I did feel a call to action; to somehow use the tools I had gained, however naïve my feeble efforts might be. If I were to remain in Japan, I would have to find a way to publicly counter the officially orchestrated war hysteria with words of compassion and understanding. On a trip to the detached temple of Minobu in Tokyo with several junior monks, I entered Hibaya Park, just outside the walls of the Imperial Palace, and found a spot in the plaza where the traffic of pedestrians converged. With the junior monks holding a banner, which read "Namu Myoho-renge-kyo", I began to preach peace. Peace depends on one's state of awareness: Within the turmoil and warmongering that appears on the surface, there is a land of harmony wherein good people worked to ease tensions and resolve conflicts. I exhorted the passersby to uproot the hatred that was being cultivated by propagandists and instead to sow understanding among their families and friends. I emphasized that President Roosevelt was not mad and didn't want war.

It didn't take long to draw a crowd, and a few moments later, plainclothes police appeared and led me away to headquarters of the Tokyo police. I was held for several hours and questioned with new intensity. When I was released that afternoon, I went directly to the American embassy and reported the incident.

It was a very disturbing series of events and left me very

nearly resolved to abandon my goals to stay and become a priest. The focus of my monastic training at that point was the teaching of Kannon, the all compassionate one, "regarder of the cries of the world"; but outside the monastery, the Japanese Imperial military and propaganda machines were exhibiting the opposite of compassion.

It was in this mood that I spent a restless night in a friend's house near the river in the village of Minobu. In the morning, I was awakened by the screams of a rat. It sounded to me as if the rat was calling to me for help. I rushed outside to find two villagers with a rat in a wire cage trap, carrying it down to the river to drown it. I ran to them and pleaded with them to show compassion and release it, quoting from the teaching of Kannon. They agreed to let it go and as they did and it scampered away, I realized that some door within my internal conflict had been opened as well. I could return to America and still be a Buddhist priest; they were not mutually exclusive ideas. I would continue in my vows and studies, and return to Japan and Minobu when it was possible. I credited the rat for recalling me to my vows, and saving me from drowning in my own cage.

Still, it was not easy to leave, and in May 1941, I made two trips to Yokohama with my trunks packed for departure, only to return to Minobu. On the third trip, I did in fact depart, with the blessing of the Lord Abbot and the promise that I could return when possible to complete my training.

With each illumination I gained, the world offered a greater darkness. The Buddha had renounced the world to understand the truth of sickness, old age, suffering and death: I had renounced materialism in favor of a deeper knowledge, and through my choices, I was going to learn of racism, suspicion, war, hate, brutality, starvation, treachery, injustice and persecution. From the mud, the lotus grows.

Chapter Three

Fates on the Wind

I should begin to talk about Iva Toguri here, though I wouldn't meet her for another two years. The childhood experiences and aspirations of two young Americans from California could hardly have been less similar. Eventually we would be thrown together and placed in the surreal limelight of a wartime propaganda machine, but about this time, we were crossing the ocean in opposite directions.

Born July 4, 1916, Iva was a Los Angeles girl whose Japanese ancestry was only a footnote to her upbringing. Her parents had emigrated from Yamanshi prefecture in Japan early in the 1900's and were determined to raise their children to be Americans. They pointedly avoided the narrow outlook of Japanese community and business associations. They characteristically chose to live in Caucasian neighborhoods, attended Christian church and Sunday school and celebrated Easter, the Fourth of July and Christmas in the traditional American ways. They had no aspiration to send their children to study in Japan, as was the custom for successful Japanese immigrant families, and from the time the children were of school age; English was the dominant language in their home.

Iva grew up a typical American girl; educated in the public schools, participated in the Girl Scouts, was active in high school athletics, took piano lessons. She had a crush on Jimmy Stewart. She had no interest in Japan, Japanese language, culture or customs; no concept of Japanese history, geography or religion; and no taste for Japanese food.

She majored in Zoology at UCLA and when she graduated in 1940, she continued in a graduate program she had hoped would lead to a medical career.

It was a family matter that took Iva to Japan. Iva's mother's only living sister had diabetes and high blood pressure and lay gravely ill in Japan. The family wished to send their love and most likely their last respects. Iva's mother was also very weak and bedridden from the same congenital ailments. Her father and brother were busy with the family retail business, and so it fell to Iva the responsibility of representing her family by her dying aunt's bedside.

It was the late spring of 1941, and hurried arrangements were made for the trip. Iva's passport was applied for and passage booked aboard the Arabia Maru, Los Angeles to Tokyo, departing July 5, as early as she could arrange.

The Toguri family had taken little interest in politics and world affairs and had no inkling of the increasingly hostile relations between Japan and the U.S. As the date of her departure drew near, there was a delay in the issuing of her passport but she was told she could obtain it from the U.S. Embassy in Tokyo after she arrived. It seemed like a small matter at the time. A bureaucratic matter, "OK…just pick it up over there".

*   *   *   *   *

As Iva waited for her ship to sail for Japan, I was reluctantly returning to California, my monastic studies cut short by the impending crisis. The passengers aboard the Ruth Alexander from Yokohama to Seattle in May 1941 were mainly refugees of one sort or another. Like me, some were Americans who had been living in Japan pressured to leave by the U.S. Embassy. There were a number of German Jews having fled their country to escape persecution there. Japan had made an unfortunate and opportunistic alliance with the Axis powers and those fleeing the European regimes we forced to move on from their temporary refuge. There was a family of Russians who had been living in Manchuria until the Japanese Imperial Army had thrown that area into turmoil through their invasion. The father had been a choirmaster at one of the large churches during the Czarist regime and they had fled Russia at the time of the Communist takeover and had settled in Manchuria. The son, Donat Ivanosky, had been born in Manchuria and spoke English as well as Russian and Chinese. He was going to the United States under the patronage of the Countess Tolstoi, who had been living in New York for years. We were an exotic mix, being swept about by historic currents,

The ship had taken a Northern route in order to call at Vancouver before it reached Seattle. It was an extremely rough crossing, so much so that through the night, people were running fore and aft below decks with flashlights to see if the steel plates of the hull were still holding together. The ship would roll and shudder, the stern of the ship would come out of the water and the propellers spun faster in the air. Then, all this steel tonnage smacked down again and the torque of the spinning screws digging into the water would shake the whole vessel from end to end. It was a terrifying crossing.

Finally we docked at Vancouver, British Columbia, and representatives of the U.S. State Department came aboard to question a number of people. One of the names on the list, wouldn't you know, was John Provoo. I was interviewed at length about where I had been and what I had been doing and they were particularly interested in what I thought about the likelihood of war in the Pacific. I gave them my candid opinion.

It seemed obvious, very obvious, I said, that war was imminent. Japan was an armed camp. The military was in control of foreign policy, and their ambitions are being thwarted by American sanctions. The children were being drilled in the art of bayoneting on their playgrounds with wooden weapons and straw enemies. The people are being told that the Americans are responsible for the hunger and shortages wracking the country. Every family had members in the military. Japan had made an alliance with the Axis Powers and the average Japanese citizen believed that war was inevitable. I repeated this story whenever asked by any member of the American government, but it always seemed to fall on deaf ears. Perhaps they knew but weren't letting on. It was strange, the Embassy in Tokyo knew war was coming, but different agencies of the government did not. The American public was more focused on our rising involvement in Europe, all the while a military build-up swirled all around the west coast ports and shipbuilding facilities of the San Francisco Bay. Of course there would be war with Japan.

In a short while, the ship sailed for Seattle. Sweet Antoinette met me there. Our friendship had become romance. I remember we attended a performance of the opera Madame Butterfly in Seattle before returning to San Francisco.

San Francisco had changed markedly in the eighteen months that I been in Japan. The anti-oriental hostility roiled closer to the surface. The people were arousing themselves to a passion for war. Most openly favored joining the war against Nazi Germany, and undoubtedly the war would include its Japanese ally as well.

I was being tossed about these currents as was most of my generation, though not in the unreasonable hatreds of Japanese and German individuals or even their countries, but swept up in the tide of patriotism and the call to duty. It was inescapable.

When I returned home, there was a draft notice waiting for me. My mother said that it had arrived a few days earlier. I took the advice to enlist rather than be drafted. Later that week I went to the Naval Intelligence Office in San Francisco and reported the fact that I had just been to the Far East and that I spoke fluent Japanese and offered my enlistment. I never received a response to this offer and as the date of my induction neared, I opted to enlist in the Army. Now, I had the naïve idea that I might be able to choose the theater of service and my assignment. I chose the quartermaster corps, which I thought consisted of issuing cases of beans and blankets and clerical duties. At any rate, I assumed it would be far from the front lines. Oh, brother.

I was sent immediately to Fort McDowell at Angel Island

in the San Francisco Bay. It was a staging area for shipment of troops overseas. I wasn't given one day's basic training, use of firearms, none of that. Instead, I was given a lot of KP. Due to the number of troops passing through Angel Island, there was a huge consolidated mess, where meals were served almost continuously except for very late at night.

Within the military's realm, the heat of war fever was more intense than with the public at large. Thousands of recruits swarmed through such facilities as Angel Island from all parts of the country; new haircuts, fresh uniforms, brave boasts and vitriolic denunciations of their probable enemies, the Germans, Italians and Japanese. In San Francisco, soldiers and sailors enjoyed their few last tastes of American entertainment; everywhere the sidewalks and bars were cluttered with young men in uniform. Young girls blushed with admiration, old men offered backslapping encouragement and nightclub emcees proposed toasts to the soon-to-be "fighting men".

In June, on a short leave, I eloped with Antoinette to Reno, Nevada and we were married before a retired Justice. We spent a few days informing friends and parents, spent a night in the Ben Franklin Hotel in San Mateo. In the morning, we raced to San Francisco to catch my boat back to Angel Island. I arrived at the dock after the boat was untied and pulling away. I had to jump and catch the rail and was pulled aboard by other GI's. This was the full extent of my marriage until 1946.

It was only a few days later that my own contingent of troops was to sail for the Philippines, and I next saw her standing on the dock and me at the rail of my ship. Since most of the troops aboard ship were from the deep South, and had no one seeing them off, an officer, the chaplain, who had became aware that my family was there at dockside, allowed me to run down the gangplank and say farewell and exchange parting embraces and run back up, and the ship cast off. A little more than five weeks before, I had been a Buddhist priest in Japan and now I was aboard ship, a married man, a U.S. Army private, embarking from San Francisco to the South Pacific.

We sailed aboard the luxury liner, the SS President Cleveland, which had been pressed into service as a troop transport. In the hurried preparations to add manpower to the American military presence in the Philippines, there was no time to spend refitting the ship, so I sailed off to war in a first class cabin with sheets on the bed. With the exception of the food, we were going to enjoy a luxury ocean voyage.

The mood aboard ship was an odd mixture of South Pacific cruise and fatalistic camaraderie. Many on board were in a similar position as myself, with little or no basic training or knowledge of military procedures. We felt that we were going to war and that we would most certainly be killed in the jungle and there was nothing to be done about it, so we might as well enjoy the boat ride.

There was almost a festive air about it. There was a large American flag painted on the side and the ship was floodlit at night during our crossing. I joined a few others in putting out a mimeographed ship's paper for the troops. We would get news from the ship's radio operator, draw up a cover with a hula girl on it, and print it up. The officer who was directing the effort gave the staff such glowing letters of commendation that it seemed we deserved instant promotion.

The ship stopped a few days in Honolulu and we were able to get off and stretch our legs for a few hours before continuing on to Manila. After the ship pulled out to sea again, I was called by the commander of troops and informed that he had received orders concerning me by radio from Washington, D.C. I was to be transferred from Quartermaster Corps to the Intelligence Department of the G-2 office at Fort Santiago, the headquarters of the Philippine Department. I, like the others, had abandoned myself to a cipher's death on some distant battlefield: a bullet flying through the air, then, lights out, game over. For some, it would be that simple. For me, it was complicated from the very beginning.

Chapter Four

Pearl of the South Pacific

Our luxury liner slid into Manila Bay, led by a pilot vessel through the mined channel between the thick jungle of the Bataan Peninsula to the north and the beautiful island of Corregidor centered in the mouth of the bay's entrance. On Corregidor, we could see large Spanish-arched buildings, manicured golf courses, scores of luxurious homes and the concrete abutments of many fortifications among the trees. Across the huge bay lay the sprawling city of Manila.

Manila in 1941 was a cosmopolitan nexus for foreign nationals. It was an open port. To us, the newly arrived troops, it was beautiful, tropical and exotic. We were quartered in the port area near the mouth of the Passig River. We hadn't really been in the military before this and there was even an enjoyable newness to Army routine.

Another shipload of new recruits would arrive in Manila almost every week, each contingent aboard a commandeered luxury liner. GI's who had arrived just weeks before were by then old timers who could direct our new comrades to the various delights of our South Pacific playground. The American dollars we had to spend could buy virtually anything in the Philippines' depressed economy. Entertaining the

American forces was rapidly becoming the biggest industry in the capital. Business in the bars, restaurants, dancehalls and brothels was feverishly booming. The enlisted men rollicked in the seamy, steamy honky-tonks, while the plethora of aging officers steeped themselves in an antiquated fantasy of colonial indulgence, "white man's burden" and "noblesse oblige".

I was assigned initially to clerical duties at the headquarters company and issued a .45 automatic that I was required to wear while on duty. Since age 14, I had considered myself to be a Buddhist priest. It had been my object to serve relations between East and West and build a world of mutual respect, reciprocity and peace; and I was saddened in the realization that I was in a position of serving the antithesis of that ideal. Although fully aware that I was under the Articles of War, I was determined to retain and protect my spiritual integrity through the most difficult of circumstances. I did not, in fact, ever fire a weapon at another human being.

Of course I had brought with me my treasured Buddhist robes. I hung them openly in my wall locker, and on Sundays I would go to the Hongwanji Temple in Manila and take along whichever Army friends were interested. I never made any attempt to hide these activities and I was unaware at the time, that such acts were the beginnings of suspicions about me.

There were many distractions about Manila to interest young American GI's. There was a great palatial glass jai alai pavilion where Filipino, and often Spanish and South American teams were the objects of enthusiastic gambling. Of the several nightclubs operated by Japanese business interests, the most popular among the GI's was the Miyako. It was not uncommon, however, for fistfights to break out between

American personnel and the Japanese men who either worked there or were patrons there for the same entertainment as the GI's. I would go there often in my early days in Manila, for the exotic entertainment and Japanese food. When a fistfight would start, I would feel compelled to intercede. It got so that every time I went out, the fights were becoming angrier, and my interventions more unwelcome, by all participants. It was rehearsal for a role that I would play under more deadly circumstances six months later. The increasingly hostile atmosphere was dismaying and I stopped going.

For the first two months at Fort Santiago, I was Private Provoo with a regular desk job filing reports on suspected subversives and known enemy agents. They were called 201 files. While working at headquarters I frequently saw General MacArthur, General Wainwright, General Sutherland and other officers of the high command. It was common talk in these quarters that Americans were making daily flights over Japanese held territory and sending photographic missions over Taiwan. Of course it was also common knowledge that American and Japanese forces had had some minor engagements although no formal state of belligerency existed.

The American 4th Marines had been stationed in Tientsin, China and had been withdrawn to the Philippines shortly before the Japanese forces arrived. They were at this time stationed at Cavite, the U.S. Naval base just south of Manila, within Manila Bay. Out here in the westernmost part of the Pacific, war with Japan, as seen by these Marines, was just around the corner, a fight postponed. I got to know some of them. They knew what was coming.

Fatefully, in my explorations of Manila, I happened to

meet Wallace Ince, an American who at the time was the top English language broadcaster in the Philippines. We had many encounters in prewar Manila, and our conversations centered on our shared backgrounds in radio. In time, Ince appears as one of the key actors in this incomprehensible drama. At the time it was simple conversations. Before the war would be over, our scripts would become of the utmost importance.

In August of 1941, I was called in to see Col. Englehardt, who was in charge of the Counter Intelligence Corps (CIC), and asked to take part in an undercover assignment. I was to pose as Jean-Paul, the ne'er-do-well son of a non-existent wealthy American family, a bon vivant trying to stay out of the way of the wartime draft, and insinuate myself into Manila "society". My objectives were to find out what people were talking about, what they were thinking, and report back.

I was provided with a number of custom tailored suits and other trappings of the role and moved into the Manila Hotel, overlooking Manila Bay, where General MacArthur occupied the penthouse suite. I played tennis, looked rich, appeared to drink heavily, and socialized. I say appeared, because drinking had been part of the problem in the radio days in San Francisco, and I needed to have my wits about me, I had to discipline myself. Aside from that, it was not difficult to play the part convincingly.

One of the places that I frequented in this guise was the Old Europe Cafe on the beautiful tree-lined Isaace Peral Street. It was run by a German family and served excellent German food. For that reason it was popular among the numerous foreigners in Manila. It was common for the patrons to be a mixture of German, French, Italian and White Russians. I managed to get myself invited to embassy parties and parties given by Axis people and attended by prominent Filipinos and wealthy sugar magnates. It was the openly expressed opinion at many of these gatherings that the American leadership was either deliberately or clumsily manipulating the Japanese to the brink of war. Roosevelt's economic sanctions and the freezing of Japanese assets had left little room for non-military options. It was felt that this was being done with indifference to the interests of the Philippine nation and that ultimately, U.S. policy would lead to the sacrifice of thousands of Filipino lives. It was also believed that in the event of war, that the Americans would not be able to hold the Philippines; not with their green untrained troops and their paunchy peacetime officers. When the Philippines fell to the Japanese, most of the plantation owners and wealthy businessmen would be willing to make a bargain with the conquerors.

I reported these comments just as I had heard them, but my superiors questioned them on several occasions. I stood by my reports. I had been a nervous and reluctant agent. I disliked the duplicity of that kind of work and several weeks after it became clear that my reports were not being received at face value, I asked to be reassigned. By November, I was Private Provoo again. My new assignment was with the Adjutant General's office, which was under the direction of Col. J.T. Menzies. My immediate superior was Captain Bishop. I was back to clerical work, typing and filing the paperwork of Army personnel matters: the arrival of various troops and their assignments.

December 8, 1941 a squadron of 54 medium sized Japanese naval bombers thundered across Manila Bay. I was with other members of the Adjutant General staff outside on the lawn looking up to see what it was. Someone near me said, "Oh boy, look at the reinforcements we're getting," then the bombs started exploding and everyone knew it had begun. Cavite, the large Naval and Marine base across a small bay from the headquarters area, was hit the hardest. December 7, across the dateline in Hawaii, the attack on Pearl Harbor had begun at the same time.

That day was the very first day that I ever touched an army rifle. It was all in pieces still packed in Cosmoline grease. We hadn't the slightest idea how to load it, shoot it or take it apart, let alone put it together.

*   *   *   *   *

In the fall of 1941, Iva Toguri was finding herself very much out of place in Japan. The smallest details of life were awkward to her; eating with chopsticks, removing her shoes upon entering a house, sitting cross-legged on the floor, the constant bowing that is virtually part of the language, and the language itself. Her command of spoken Japanese was less than rudimentary, and she could not read at all. It made it worse that she looked Japanese. A college graduate in California, here, she was virtually illiterate. Although she felt very warmly toward her Aunt's family, contact with the rest of Japanese society was extremely uncomfortable. She enrolled in a school that specialized in acculturating foreigners to Japanese life.

There were shortages of everything in the winter of 1941, from food and clothing to heating fuel. The thing that was heating up was the official anti-foreigner campaign and warlike sentiments. Her arrival in Japan had come just one day before President Roosevelt had frozen all Japanese assets in the United States and increased the extent of the U.S. economic blockade of strategic materials. With winter coming on several months later, the economic squeeze was beginning to be painfully felt.

It became clear to Iva that she did not want to be in Japan, but with her passport held up by interminable red tape, she could not readily depart. She had booked passage back to the U.S. aboard a ship departing December 2, 1941, but was not allowed to board because she lacked the proper papers.

When the war began a few days later, Iva was stranded.

Chapter Five

White, Yellow, Orange and Red

I was just a young man of 24, and naïve of course in many ways, but this attack came as little surprise to me. As anticipated by a broad range of Asia experts, military planners and journalists, the Japanese would attempt to extend their Pacific empire to include the oil-rich Dutch East Indies. Ernest Hemingway, arriving in Manila from China in the spring of 1941 had made exactly this assessment and also the prediction that the Japanese forces would attack the Philippines before the American garrison there was made so strong that it would be impossible. My own slapdash mustering had been a part of a hurried buildup of U.S. forces that was both preparing for and bringing on the attack.

Capture of the Philippines was the Japanese immediate objective in beginning the war with the U.S. The attack on Pearl Harbor was a pre-emptive strike on the American naval capability, and an attempt to get the Americans to first consider defenses closer to home.

To the public in the U.S., and even to the majority of the enlisted men in the Philippines, this inevitable confrontation was portrayed as unlikely, since Japan was such a small, poor country, it would never undertake attacking the greatest military power on earth. When it did come, that attack was described as a totally unexpected and baffling act of Japanese treachery.

To professional military planners, the attack had been a contingency anticipated at least since 1926, when students at the Philippine War College were first offered details of the Orange Plan. "Orange" was a code word for Japan. It was assumed that the Japanese would make an amphibious invasion in the Lingayen Gulf to the Northwest of Luzon and advance on Manila from the North...which they did. The Orange Plan called for the withdrawal of American Forces and the Philippine Scouts to the Bataan Peninsula and the fortified islands of Manila Bay...which they did. Those forces were expected to be able to hold out until the U.S. Navy arrived ...which they did not. The Japanese, aware of the details of the Orange Plan, had crippled the U.S. fleet at Pearl Harbor, 5,000 miles away, and the planned rescue would never come, leaving the defenders of Bataan and Corregidor to fight with what little we had.

And I had another perspective from which to anticipate the war. I had been in Japan just six months before and had gotten a full dose of the government's efforts to prepare their civilian population for war with the West. The attitude of the average citizen had become one of open hostility ...they were being backed into a corner, being literally starved, and their economy strangled. Everywhere there had been posters of foreigners depicted as barbaric monsters, and Uncle Sam as an evil menacing giant. I had attempted to get this across to my superiors at counter intelligence, but my reports to this effect were not welcomed. More than a decade later, I would discover that these reports were not being received as military intelligence, but as indications of my own potential disloyalty.

The Philippine Department was overstaffed with older, higher ranking officers for whom it had been a rather cushy station. Many were approaching retirement age and spending their last years enjoying the comfortable quarters and the numerous golf courses. They could even escape the tropical heat among the pines at Little Baguio and Lake Taal. It was as if their mission were to staff a South Pacific country club.

As for experienced combat troops, or even trained troops, we were woefully understaffed. Many, like me, had never had a day's basic training. We had been drafted, packed aboard ships and sent off as part of a frantic effort to "reinforce" the Philippine Department. Efforts had been made to train the Philippine Army, and it must be said, to their credit, that the Philippine Scouts were well trained, unquestionably loyal, and a great asset to the American Forces. Much had been done in the area of planning but little in the area of implementation. As far as military hardware, ammunition, supply and the preparedness of their combat personnel, the situation was pitiful in the face of the formidable onslaught of the Japanese war machine that was coming.

December 8, the planes appeared in the skies approaching Manila. It wasn't until the bombs started exploding we realized they were not our own. The city went into an immediate blackout, sentries were posted everywhere, and American Forces went into the initial stages of Orange Plan; the withdrawal to the Bataan Peninsula across the bay from Manila and to the fortified islands in the bay's entrance, the largest of which is Corregidor. The plan was to spare the civilian population of Manila by declaring it an open city and removing all military targets. Munitions were moved by every means to stockpiles on Corregidor and Mariveles, just across the north channel of the bay's entrance on the tip of the Bataan Peninsula.

By now, I was a corporal, and my duties on the Adjutant General's staff were to hurriedly burn records, pack field desks and gather equipment needed to set up headquarters in the field.

It was quite apparent that the Japanese were going follow their air assault with a land invasion somewhere in the Philippine Islands and they did arrive as anticipated, 100 miles north of Manila on the Lingayen Gulf, in order to sweep down the Pampangas Plain and attack Manila and Bataan by land.

My unit began our evacuation of Fort Santiago and boarded a tug to be taken across the bay. When we first landed on the island of Corregidor, there hadn't been any destruction. It was very beautiful and covered with trees. It had many, many beautiful buildings, comfortable quarters and well kept parade grounds.

Corregidor is about three miles long with one fat end about a mile across, narrowing down to a point at the other end, shaped rather like a comma, or a pollywog, the fat end toward the mouth of the bay and the South China Sea. At its crest was Topside Barracks, known as the longest concrete barracks in the world; nearby was the Middleside Barracks, somewhat smaller. Further down the island about in the middle of its length is a bulge, Malinta Hill, which contains a huge tunnel complex called Malinta Tunnel. The tunnels were designed to accommodate and maintain the enormous railway-track-mounted naval guns that were for the purpose of defending Manila Bay from attack by sea, which was unfortunate since they could not be brought to bear on the Japanese who would eventually reach it coming from overland, down the Bataan Peninsula. The biggest guns were virtually useless.

We set up the Adjutant General's office in the Middleside Barracks in what formerly had been a day room. They had filing cabinets and desks, and we had brought our typewriters and there still were some pool tables. We were well established by Christmas, and they were able to get together a real Christmas dinner, with a turkey from the States and all the trimmings. For the moment, we were able to forget the bloody confrontation that was bearing down on us; we were even able to believe for the moment that Corregidor was an impregnable fortress and that the Japanese wouldn't even dare fly over. That illusion lasted until December 29 when the Japanese not only flew over it, but they bombed nearly every building and gun emplacement on the island. The railway on which the big guns were moved never operated again. War became a reality for me that day.

I was in the day room taking dictation from Col. Menzies when I heard the clanging. Someone had begun banging on some empty brass shell casings to indicate that an air raid was coming. Bombs began to explode and the Colonel and I made a dash for the small kitchen that was used for the Colonel's quarters. We hit the doorway at the same time and for a second, neither of us could get through. The colonel dived onto his cot and the I dived under it. Bombs exploded outside, nearby and all around. Bombs crashed into Middlesides

Barracks, doing considerable damage. As the bombing let up briefly, we ran outside to find better shelter. I remember this as my company's initiation to war; and in the frenzied search for shelter, we freshmen ran every which way, as organized as ants on a burning log.

Colonel Menzies and I ran up the hill toward Topsides Barracks, crouching low in the ravines. We stopped at several anti-aircraft positions on the way, some of them not being operated yet. The anti-aircraft equipment that was there was pitiful relative to the situation. The nose cones of the anti-aircraft shells had to be set by hand by turning some dials so that they would go off at a given altitude ...which was ludicrous in the face of these very rapidly flying bombers diving straight at us. At one of the gun emplacements, the man who was supposedly to operate the range finder was not in place yet, if he was still alive, and I found myself doing the job, something I had previously known nothing about whatsoever. In that chaotic day the Colonel and I moved our locations four times.

During our next move, the planes began diving and we ran into a low culvert that ran under a road. It was crammed full of people. Someone said, "Do you know what we're laying in?" An officer in front of me said, "Yes, shit!" We squished down lower in the flow of sewage that ran beneath us as more bombs burst and the ground shook.

The bombing let up and again we were out on open ground and running. This time we ran into a short tunnel where there had been some excavating to build garages for some officers' homes. They had not been completed and they were shored up with heavy timbers. Many people were lined up against either side. The bombs were falling very close. One bomb came down a small residence just across the road where some Filipino workmen had taken refuge. It was blown completely apart and shrapnel rang through the entrance of the tunnel where we were hiding and many people on the other side of the tunnel were hit.

Everywhere there was the overwhelming smell of the burnt explosives, so thick that we could hardly catch our breaths. It seemed so intense an air raid that at times we felt like no one could be left alive except us.

Of course many, many were killed that day, but many survived as well. Finally it was over. It grew quiet and hundreds of us crept from whatever shelter that had been found in a terrified moment. Hundreds of bodies were being lined up near the entrance to Malinta Tunnel, and hundreds more wounded were being carried in, in basket-like stretchers.

Everyone joined in the sorting out the unconscious and the wounded from the dead. I found myself carrying bodies to a central location, and saying a short Buddhist prayer over each one.

Two days later, our unit was packing to move headquarters to the Bataan Peninsula. We put our field desks and file cabinets, as well as our personal things and barracks bags, on barges for the move. We had planned to leave very early the next morning to land at Cabcaben, but by the time the tug pulled away from the dock it was ten o'clock in the morning and the Japanese subjected our flotilla to intermittent strafing. In the confusion with me diving between the desks and filing cabinets for cover, my barracks bag was lost over the side and with it my Buddhist robes.

The 4000-foot volcanic peaks of the Mariveles Mountains run down through the center of the Bataan Peninsula dividing it into an East and West sector. Over 100,000 people were on the Bataan Peninsula; 20,000 American soldiers, 10,000 Philippine Army, and 30,000 civilians who had taken this dubious refuge. Bearing down on them from the north was General Homma's 14th Army; 43,000 well supplied, battle hardened Japanese soldiers. The U.S. military airplanes had been all but eliminated on December 8th, but the Japanese had at least 100 bombers and many more fighters, and were constantly being resupplied throughout the campaign.

My unit had set up headquarters at the base of some enormous jungle trees at the foot of the mountains. With the help of faithful Filipinos, we dug out some elaborate bomb shelters, covered them over with large branches and camouflaged canvas, so that one could scarcely detect an entrance from ten feet away. The Japanese were flying a photographic mission over the peninsula mid morning each day, and in the early afternoon the bombers would come over and drop a token number of bombs in our general area before continuing on to more thoroughly bomb Corregidor.

At night we were able to pick up radio broadcasts from Manila, and from "the Voice of Freedom" on Corregidor, staffed by Captain Wallace Ince, the radio announcer I had met in Manila, now a Captain in the Army. Some times we were able to pick up broadcasts from San Francisco wherein we received a great deal of praise and encouragement for holding our position. That was great for morale, giving us the impression that we were not, as we were, isolated and without hope of rescue. William Wintner, broadcasting from San Francisco's Fairmont Hotel, 5,000 miles away, dared the Japanese to attack Bataan and Corregidor. And you know, in those days everyone listened to the radio. It wasn't our imaginations; challenges were often followed by heavier shelling.

The Japanese, by that time had full control of the sea and air, and their ground troops were closing in. The Mariveles Mountains were considered an area through which the Japanese could not easily penetrate, but they did, even bringing down heavy artillery pieces through extremely difficult terrain. A vise was being tightened on both sectors.

Very late one night our unit got word that the Japanese had landed a force of about 400 troops at Agaloma Point which lay behind us between the headquarters and the Bay proper, but the next report was that it was 4000 troops that had not only landed but were firmly entrenched. We had nothing to meet this with except some rear echelon troops and headquarters companies' personnel. We had no real front line battle experience. It was necessary to call down some very badly needed tank battalions from the main battle front and in the resulting battle they blasted away all the trees and foliage from the point and nearly all the Japanese. The last several hundred invading troops lept over the cliffs and down onto the rocks where they were killed in a suicidal fall. A small contingent of Japanese had taken refuge in a cave on the cliff's face and the engineers swung a large dynamite charge inside and detonated it. At the end of this battle, I saw to my further horror, the badly wounded and dying enemy troops having their teeth kicked out and their bodies looted for the various charms and souvenirs that they wore, by American and Filipino soldiers.

American and Japanese forces were engaged at such close range that the wires of their field telephones even got crossed and I could hear the enemy talking back and forth when it was my turn to man the field switchboard. The lighted switchboard had been an extremely hazardous duty station at night and several operators had been killed by Japanese sniper fire. When my turn came, I memorized the panel so that I could operate it in the dark.

It was shortly after the battle at Agoloma Point that I had one of my most terrifying experiences of the war. I had traded my .45 automatic for a pair of revolvers, which I was hoping not to have to use, but in the Army, you are required to be armed. I was lying in my little shelter at the root of a large tree, sort of half asleep and I opened my eyes and could see dimly through the mosquito net, the face of a Japanese soldier not more than six inches from my face. I could see clearly the star on the cap and expected to feel the thrust of his saber at any second. I grabbed one of my pistols and fired at the figure crouching near my bunk, and then, in the moonlight then I could see that it was a large ape rushing out of my shelter. Thankfully, I didn't hit it. The shot went through the roof of the colonel's tent just down the hill. Someone started clanging on the empty oil drum and aroused the whole camp. I didn't know it at the time, but I was in the initial stages of cerebral malaria. It was the only time I ever fired a gun at a living being; I was armed and delirious.

The next day I was in a sorrier state with a high fever and was taken away to a field hospital, which was actually a series of crude beds outdoors, the only area that was covered was the surgical area. They had only a limited amount of quinine for the treatment of malaria and no Atabrine to reduce fever. Beside each bed a foxhole had been dug for use during air raids. One of the chief dangers in this location was the falling unexploded shells of our own antiquated anti-aircraft batteries from the Island of Corregidor. They would fire toward the Japanese bombers as they approached over the Bataan Peninsula. At one time while I was in the hospital, the patient next to me rolled out of bed and into his foxhole and one of these nose cones came directly through his back. I wasn't able to get out of my bed at the time but I wasn't touched.

One day while I was still recuperating, I was recognized by a courier from my own headquarters company, who told me that our unit was going to move that day. I climbed on the back of the courier's motorcycle, still dressed in my hospital garb. I couldn't let myself become permanently separated from my company. It was fortunate that I did because as it turned out, we were moving back to Corregidor.

We spent the day packing the equipment up and trucking it down to the now ruined town of Cabcaben beside the bay. There was only room for the equipment and the ranking staff aboard the available boats and barges, and I was left behind. As night fell it became obvious that there was no easy way back to Corregidor so I made my way across the mined and shark infested three-mile stretch of the North Channel on the trunk of a palm tree with two other soldiers. It took us all night to get there. As we approached North Mine dock in the darkness, a searchlight flickered on to see what was approaching. Bodies were floating here and there in the water and there were other people trying to get across. Many had been eaten by sharks.

Looking back across the channel we could see the town of Cabcaben in flames and from the tracer bullets of the machine gun fire there, it was clear that the Japanese had completely overrun the peninsula.

Chapter Six

The Rock

With General King's surrender of American and Filipino forces on Bataan, April 9th, the Japanese were able to concentrate their efforts on the island fortress of Corregidor to complete their conquest of the Philippines and eliminate the American military from its strategic position. It would have been easy enough to accomplish that by siege and blockade. Over 14,000 people crowded onto the island, and the forces there had been on half rations for some time and now we had been cut further, down to the lower limits of human survival. Supplies could hold out for barely more than a month at the most.

General Homma, commander of the Japanese forces, however, needed a more spectacular military victory to restore his honor following several embarrassing setbacks on Bataan. He wished to further establish the reputation of the Imperial Army in decisive combat. He had been provided a large quantity of new artillery pieces and by April 11th had 150 artillery batteries in place at the end of the Bataan peninsula and on the shores of Cavite to the south. In addition to their already sizeable Air Force, they brought in sixty new bombers. They began a bombardment that lasted 27 days that turned the island into a smoldering junk pile. Knowing how placid and green it was when we arrived, it seemed we were living in the corpse of that vision, and everything smelt of death, of sewage, of burnt explosives.

During the months that battle raged on Bataan, on Corregidor we had been subjected to a daily routine of regular air bombardment. That was, in relative terms, livable. A photo-reconnaissance plane flew over at high altitude each day in the late morning. In the early afternoon the bombing would begin on the selected targets. It was livable in the sense that it was on schedule. Meals and activities outside the bomb shelters and tunnels could be arranged, and at the appointed hour, with the exception of the antiaircraft personnel and the Marines dug in on the beaches, the inhabitants of Corregidor could come out of our burrows in the lulls between the rain of bombs. That lasted until the Japanese had finished with Bataan.

For a short while, I was quartered in the bombed-out shell of the old theater building. There was also a large monkey who had taken refuge, who no longer had a desire to live outside. I would go to work inside Malinta Tunnel each day to work at the Adjutant General's office and return to the theater at night. One evening when I returned, the building was completely gone, not a trace of it remained. From then on, I lived inside the tunnel, sleeping on my desk.

Malinta Tunnel is rather a labyrinth of tunnels beneath Malinta Hill. The main tunnel is about a quarter of a mile long, like a large streetcar tunnel running completely through the hill. It was 30 feet across at the base and 20 feet high in the middle, and reinforced with concrete. Off the main tunnel there are 23 lateral tunnels, slightly smaller in height and width, each about 150 feet long. One of these lateral tunnels leads to the north into another complex of tunnels that comprised the hospital, originally designed for a maximum of 300 patients. The hospital complex had its own opening to the North. Still another lateral leads off the main tunnel to the South through the quartermasters 11 tunnels into the 4 Navy tunnels, housing the small Navy staff, headquarters for the 4th Marines, and radio broadcast facilities. The tunnel complex is deep enough underground to be truly bombproof. As more and more realized that it was the one of the few genuine havens from bombardment and certainly the largest, the numbers taking shelter inside grew and grew, until by the time that the end came, over 4000 had taken up residence inside, and 1000 more were crammed into the hospital. Beside the Malinta tunnel complex, there were innumerable smaller caves, tunnels and ammunition storage areas on the island that were far enough underground to offer shelter.

With no other task before them, the Japanese concentrated their firepower in a total devastation of the surface of Corregidor. The shelling would begin at dawn each day and the roar of bombs and artillery shells explosions were continuous until noon, when there was a lull that became known as the "Japanese siesta". In the early afternoon, hardly an hour later, it would increase again to its morning level and continue this way until after midnight Throughout the remainder of the night shelling would be sporadic at a much reduced level, just enough to make sure no one would ever get completely asleep.

As the shelling progressed, the wounded jammed the hospital, so that many makeshift bunks had to be constructed and piled in tiers four high. Thousands of large droning flies filled the tunnel from one end to the other. The air was thick with the smell of decay and death. The tunnel's ventilation system was designed for the small number of personnel required for handling the storage of supplies and the refurbishment of artillery pieces and never meant to accommodate any appreciable number of people at all. Light and power was provided by a diesel generator at the east end of the tunnel, the lower end, and the fumes of its exhaust added their odor to the thick air. In the dimly lit tunnels, life went on, after a fashion. There were a few weddings, an occasional jam session and, of course, many funerals.

All the tunnel entrances were heavily sandbagged, and one could step outside for a breath of fresh air or a salt-water shower, but often at risk of one's life. Fresh water was in extremely short supply as the major reservoirs had been destroyed. There was no longer any fresh meat (some of the "fresh meat" had been stamped 1917, as old as I was) since the cold storage plant had been destroyed as well, after which we were reduced to small quantities canned fish, and toward the end, only red rice, half spoiled canned tomatoes and fruit salad. A mess was set up at the lower end of the tunnel. The cooking was done just inside, and tables had been set up, at standing level just outside the tunnel entrance. Many died from malnutrition and its complicating effect on tropical diseases; and many died in their weakness from minor wounds. Of course, many died of major wounds as well and many were completely blown to pieces.

Outside the tunnels, the once beautiful island looked like a cratered desert. No building remained standing and all the vegetation and wildlife had been completely blasted away.

A change was taking place in me as the fate of Corregidor became more obvious. To assimilate it all, and coming to grips with the impending doom, I had become increasingly conscious of the description of a perfect world in the Lotus Sutra. Here that thesis could be examined under the most extreme circumstances. Putting my trust in the Buddha, the Dharma and the Sangha, I found moments during the night bombardments when I felt so calmed by this, I began to leave the tunnel and walk down to a rocky promontory on the south shore and intone my chant as the bombs fell, its meaning never more vivid:

"Beneath the dark surface of this crumbling illusion,

My perfect world shimmers with light.

Though this illusion seems burning,

And these suffering beings lie broken and bleeding,

Believing the end of the kalpa is near.

My perfect peaceful world is here,

And these beings are whole and filled with light."

I did this dozens of times. And returning calmly to the safety of the tunnels after these sojourns, the M.P.'s gave me strange and ominous glares ...I must have seemed too serene and contented; and why would I leave the tunnel during air raids?

The real heroes of the siege were the 4th Marines, who through it all, had to remain in their handmade foxholes and fortifications dug into the beaches and hillsides, with horrible instant death raining all around them, constantly, for these 27 days of incessant bombardment. I had quite a few friends among them and one day, I was able to scrape up enough ingredients to make a batch of donuts with the help of some Filipino friends. I carried a big pan of them down to where the Marines were dug in near Monkey Point. On my way down the bombardment started hitting the area I was crossing. I ducked in and out of craters and foxholes and finally reached the Marines' position just at the height of the barrage. The half starved Marines could not believe their eyes. The Marines were in the worst fix of all those on Corregidor. It was the most difficult position to get food, and by that time all communications had to be done at great risk by courier. There were no ambulances running and the wounded had to be carried by stretcher often over a mile to the hospital.

General Wainwright was the commander of all the forces in the Philippines after General MacArthur had been withdrawn to Australia. In many ways he was the antithesis of General MacArthur. Where MacArthur was aloof and distant commander, aristocratic in his manner, larger than life; Wainwright was the skinny, down to earth cavalry officer, a "regular Joe", comfortable and friendly with the men. Where MacArthur was respected and even held in awe: Wainwright was genuinely loved by his men. Both were known to expose themselves to the dangers that their front line troops risked and each did it in his own characteristic way; MacArthur would appear while under fire and stride about majestically surveying the scene with an air of invincibility and hardly lose an ash off his cigar, while Wainwright would spend at least an hour outside the tunnels each day, moving from foxhole to foxhole stopping at each for a homey chat with the men in their positions. Each General considered this sort of thing an essential duty of the commander, and especially in this campaign since as Wainwright put it, "they have so damn little to fight with, at least we can give them some morale".

In the final days of Corregidor's siege, there was considerable resentment, though not toward Wainwright and those who shared their predicament. Throughout the Bataan campaign the troops listened to the radio reports of the relief convoy on its way. Gradually they had become cynical about this ever-eminent convoy. In fact, it never came. In February, when President Roosevelt addressed the nation over the radio, he spelled out the necessity, as he saw it, of concentrating on the war in Europe first. He scarcely mentioned the besieged garrison on Corregidor. From that time forward it was apparent to all that we were on our own and that no relief was coming. On March 11th, MacArthur was withdrawn by submarine to Australia. When word of this reached the ranks, we felt a pervasive sense of doom. When Bataan fell on April 9th, and pressure began to mount on the survivors on Corregidor, we felt as cornered rats, packed closer and closer together in the tunnels; sick, starving, sleepless, terrorized and worst of all abandoned and forgotten by the government we served. To me it would have been unthinkable at that time that any garrison could ever have felt a greater sense of abandonment.

On the field of battle, one gains acute awareness as to the pulse of the war. We know when something is changing, when the tempo is increasing, building up to something. On May 5th, something had changed: The bombardment was more intense than before, and we knew a new kind of attack was forming.

I was near the lower end of the tunnel and happened to be reading passages from the Christian Bible. A large bomb came down just outside the tunnel entrance where the mess tables were located and killed a large number of people who were standing there. The ground shook and dirt and rocks fell down through the cracks in the weakened concrete reinforcement of the tunnel. The words I was reading seemed to come alive on the page and swim and burn before my eyes.."...ten thousand shall fall at your right hand, but not a hair of your head shall be touched.."

It was soon thereafter that we were called together in the main tunnel. It was usually bedlam in the tunnel, like a chaotic bazaar, but now it was dead silent. General Wainwright came out and addressed all assembled. He said to prepare for an all out Japanese assault on the island. He said that all ambulatory personnel would be assigned battle stations.

The assault came that night and in the light of the full moon and the silver light of the phosphorus flares could be seen a flotilla of hundreds of barges and boats of every description approaching the island from both sides of the bay. The defenders held their fire until the Japanese drew near to more efficiently use their supply of ammunition. Then it began.

The Japanese made their landing at a low beach between Malinta Hill and Monkey Point on the tail of the island. Many of their boats were blasted out of the water by our heavy mortars and as they hit the beaches: they were taking heavy losses. Wave after wave came in, being killed by the scores. The wave following would clamber over the piles of dead and unceasingly charge into the firing, overwhelming positions by their sheer willingness to absorb bullets with their bodies. The Japanese artillery barrage preceded them slowly up the beach destroying everything in its path and the attackers pressed inland. The defenders fell back and fell back.

I had been given the post of guarding the hospital entrance, with orders to maintain its conceivably protected status under the Geneva Convention by disarming everyone entering. Scores of freshly wounded were rushed in and some who were merely in a state of hysteria, some of them officers. My job was to have them stack their rifles outside and let them enter. As the defenders on the beach fell back again and again, more and more wounded were jammed into the hospital, and the already packed Malinta Tunnel. There was already standing room only making it nearly impossible to pass through the throng. Senior officers who had been conferring with General Wainwright came through with difficulty and spread the word that he intended to surrender at noon. Japanese tanks had landed and had joined the action. It was not possible to go on; there were few heavy weapons left in the hands of the defenders that were functional and they were at Topside away from the invasion beaches on the tail of the island. The beach defenses had been annihilated, and there was no communication possible between the remaining fighting units and their headquarters. The fresh water supply was completely gone. It was only possible to surrender or pointlessly die.

At 11:00 in the morning, General Wainwright radioed his intention to surrender to President Roosevelt and General MacArthur. The message was translated and repeatedly broadcast in Japanese.

At noon, those who had received the surrender order ceased fire and began smashing their weapons. White flags were hung outside the tunnel entrances and a white flag was run up the flagpole at Topside barracks, and the American flag taken down and burned. The Japanese, however, did not slow their firing. Wainwright repeatedly radioed to the Japanese but was unable to establish communication. Finally he sent a Marine Captain out onto the battlefield with a white flag in hand. He was able to find a Japanese commander and soon there was a lull in the fighting and Generals Wainwright, Beebe and Moore were escorted through the lines.

They were taken to Bataan to meet with General Homma, at 5:00 that evening. Wainwright attempted to conceal that he was commander of all Allied Forces in the Philippines and to surrender only the besieged garrisons on Corregidor and the fortified islands of Manila Bay. The ruse was turned against him; General Homma insisted that Wainwright was the supreme commander as had been stressed again and again on the American news broadcasts. When Wainwright realized the situation, he agreed to surrender all, but Homma would not accept, since Wainwright had previously denied his authority. Homma left the meeting, saying that battle would continue. Further discussions would have to be conducted with Colonel Nakayama, the field commander on Corregidor who had accompanied the surrender party to Bataan. After much pleading the American Generals were able to persuade Nakayama to wind down the hostilities, though all those captured would remain battle captives rather than prisoners of war until all remaining forces in the Philippines actually did lay down their arms. All were to remain hostages, and therefore subject to summary execution, until this did, in fact, occur. Then and only then would we be treated as prisoners of war.

That evening, back on Corregidor, General Wainwright

made formal arrangements to send his emissaries to General Sharp on Mindinao, and to Colonel Horan operating guerrilla units in the North to persuade them to surrender.

When General Wainwright and his aides had left for Bataan to negotiate with General Homma the night before, battle was still in progress in many places and everything was in an uncertain status. There were 4000 of us inside Malinta Tunnel. We had disarmed ourselves, but outside, the fighting had not stopped and we were helpless. Our officers organized a party to proceed outside the tunnel under white flag and surrender the tunnel to the nearest Japanese officer. This was arranged and the first contingent of Japanese appeared inside the tunnel entrance. They were extremely cautious, expecting a trap.

The Japanese ordered everyone to kneel, but this was not possible since there was barely room to stand. We crushed ourselves against the walls to make a corridor so the Japanese could enter. The officers proceeded through, followed by a number of soldiers. Their sabers and bayonets dripped with the blood of our own people. They seethed with battle-crazed hatred and many of them bled from their own wounds. They had suffered enormous casualties in taking Corregidor, and we would soon learn, we were considered "battlefield captives", still in a fight that was not finished. We could be beheaded or bayoneted for the slightest misstep.

Word had reached Corregidor in the months before of the Japanese atrocities at the fall of Hong Kong and Singapore, and many feared for the nurses who might be raped and the patients that might be bayoneted in their hospital beds. In the weeks that followed, our status remained uncertain and it was clear that any organized resistance could precipitate a massacre. This did not happen, though many individuals, for little reason, were butchered in front of us, among us. There was nothing to be done about it. This was being totally at the mercy of the totally merciless.

Officers of senior rank were separated from the rest of us and led off to a lateral (a smaller side tunnel) under guard. By that time, I was Sergeant John Provoo and I was one of the 3000 plus that were herded just outside the lower entrance of the tunnel and packed into an excavated amphitheater-like area. The Japanese set up machine gun positions around us, and left a small number of nervous guards with guns trained on a helpless crowd.

Many American units on Topside continued to fight, being out of touch with their commanders. The Japanese sent their troops to meet them. The shelling from Bataan increased again and many rounds landed near where we were being held, punctuating General Homma's threats to Wainwright taking place at that moment. Fighting continued sporadically through the night and in the morning, planes bombed and strafed near the captives' area and still another artillery barrage opened up from Bataan. The shelling became so intense around us that the Japanese guarding us had to take cover and some of us huddled along the road there were wounded by shrapnel.

Finally the last holdouts realized it was over, and came down the hill from Topside holding a white flag as we cheered them. Then the first silence in over a month came to Corregidor; a stinking, ghastly silence.

Chapter Seven

The Hard Place

Any idea that the Geneva Convention would protect the 3000 held there outside the tunnel was a dangerous delusion. Those of us who were foolish enough to complain about our treatment, were answered by the blow of a rifle butt or worse. We were finally allowed to stand up and move around a little and relieve ourselves. Japanese soldiers went among us grabbing wristwatches, fountain pens and taking eyeglasses that looked like they had gold rims. They approached people at random and hit them in the face; they doubled up their fists and hit them as hard as they could on the side of the face. One had no choice but to take it. In many ways this is harder to deal with than combat, and over a period of time, the psychological effects of being helpless in the face of captors unrestrained in their whimsical cruelty are excruciating.

A month before, the captive surrendered forces on Bataan had begun their infamous Death March. Sick, starving and wounded prisoners were marched 65 miles to the north, away from the battlefront, in the hot sun, without food, water, medical help or sanitation. Those who could not keep up the pace, for whatever reason, were bayoneted where they fell. Rotting corpses lined the route, and in the end 10,000 had died along the way. The fate of a prisoner of war is perhaps the most terrible of humanity. In the hands of their victorious enemy, far from the sight of "civilized" authorities, and most often forgotten by their own government, the idea that they can respond to everything with "name, rank and serial number" is totally unrealistic.

American MP's had been pressed into service to help the Japanese control some of the movements of our surrendered troops. Several were stationed at the mouth of the tunnel. A Japanese officer came out of the tunnel, and conferred with one of them. The MP turned toward the captives down below. "Sergeant Provoo, you're wanted inside." Word was passed along through the captives and finally reached me. I was struck with a new sense of dread. The last thing one would want in such a situation was to attract any individual attention. Up until this point, I was just one of the mass of captives; now, to be singled out and called by name, could only mean trouble. I walked up the hill in the hot morning air and back into the gloom and stench where I had lived for the previous month.

I was led to a lateral where two Japanese officers were questioning two American officers. I was asked to interpret. One of the Japanese was the air commander, and one was the artillery commander. They were trying to illicit from our officers an opinion; which had been more decisive in the battle for Corregidor; the bombing or the shelling? The American officers were trying to be tactfully non-committal and I did my best to offer an ambiguous translation along the same lines. The Japanese grew bored with this after a few minutes and to my relief, sent me away. I hoped that was all there would be to it and started walking back toward the tunnel entrance, praying silently that I would be able to get back to the others outside, but I didn't make it.

Instead, I was taken by officers of the Kempeitai (the Japanese version on the Gestapo) and placed in a small lateral under close guard with a number of other prisoners. Most of the others were headquarters personnel, and at least one was a signal corps officer. They were being taken out, one at a time, some were being returned and some, ominously, were not. Outside we had become aware that there were a number of executions taking place, and now, from the reports of those being returned to the lateral, it was apparent that this place we were being held was the threshold of that fate.

It was while I was being held in this lateral that a meeting between General Wainwright and Colonel Nakayama along with several aides took place within earshot. I became aware of the General's predicament and indeed the predicament of all the captives. The captors' tone was cruel and demanding, and had not Wainwright complied totally, I am certain everyone would have been massacred.

Finally, it was my turn and I was taken to another lateral where I found myself standing before three Japanese officers who were holding interrogations, a military court of sorts. There were guards present and another man who was their interpreter. One of the officers spoke: "We know you, you are Provoo, you were in Japan less than one year ago, you are a spy!" The dossier that had been created by the Tokyo police had caught up with me. I was certain that I was doomed. I replied truthfully that I had been in Japan to study Buddhism and that I had been a novice priest at Minobu. One of the officers grunted to the guard..."KOROSU!"...Kill him. The officer in the middle intervened saying that maybe I could be telling the truth. They should hold me until my story was checked out. I was returned to the lateral where I was being held before.

It was hard to tell how long I was held after that. Within the gloomy tunnel, one could not tell day from night and in my state of mind, it could have been minutes or hours. I was taken out, my story had been checked; I would not be executed. I was led to a guard post and given an armband that said "interpreter", in Japanese characters, so that guards would know they were being understood. Then I was taken outside to rejoin the others.

The captives now numbered over 10,000 and they had been taken to an area on the beach where a concentration camp had been established. It was the 92nd garage area, which had formerly been a ramp for amphibious planes and maintenance facilities. There stood the remains of a large hanger with a shredded metal roof. Tattered pieces fell on the people when the wind blew. Most people were out on the beach with no cover at all. We had not yet been allowed to dig any latrines, or to even move about and so everyone had to relieve himself where he was. It was very, very hot and the air swarmed with millions and millions of large flies. We had no food, no water; and hundreds lay dying from dysentery, malnutrition, malaria, pellagra and dehydration. Hundreds more would follow. Some became crazed with dehydration and rushed into the sea, where they were killed. Signs posted along the water's edge said: "Anyone going into the water will be shot severely."

There were quite a number of incidents of violence usually due to the fact that the captives did not understand the guards' orders, or did not understand the rules they were required to follow, or were blind to everything that was happening around them, or insisted on being treated in accordance with the provisions of the Geneva Convention. No one was allowed even to get up off the ground after dark. If they did, they were beaten at least, and many were killed, just for that infraction.

So the task fell naturally to me to intercede whenever violence threatened. When events began to get out of hand someone would call out, "Get Sergeant Provoo, he can tell us what this guy's yelling about." I would come rushing over and then my unenviable duty was to translate the guard's harsh words and often cruel and arbitrary rules, and in so doing, would appear to be an instrument of our captor's brutality. Many times I was able to smooth things over and neutralize the hostility by a number of devices.

I had a unique status in this situation, in that nearly all the real communication between captor and captive had to pass through me. Often I used the simplest of ploys with success: I would ask the guard politely if he had any children, and almost invariably they would bring out snapshots of his little pink-faced kids back home and he would be diverted for the moment. Thus interrupted, the guard, finally returning to his duties would say "Now you tell this one that the rule is that you can't do this or go there"...or whatever the incident had arisen over, and that would be the end of it. I undoubtedly saved numerous lives in this manner, and as word spread I would be called upon almost constantly during the day, and many times every night.

Perhaps this was the destiny that all my extracurricular interests had been preparing me for, and my value as a bridge between East and West would be realized, in this most unexpected way. Now, I thought, my religious convictions and my loyalty to my fellow soldiers could be merged into one duty. Throughout the days and nights in the concentration area, potentially lethal conflicts would arise and someone would call out "Get Sergeant Provoo, quick" and I would rush to intervene. I was under intense pressure and it was having its effect on me: Perhaps it was my finest hour, or perhaps, I had to consider, I was cracking up. I had no time to contemplate which, nor an option to act differently.

Suspicion is an insidious thing. It builds on itself, silently, away from the light. Once given a premise, all events, great and small, can be bent toward the conclusion, each proven by all the misunderstanding that has come before; each new rumor adding weight to the larger narrative. Suspicion reinforced once, twice, and even evidence contrary to the premise can be given a status that it is a diversionary tactic of the suspect, and thus, further proof. In much of my childhood, I had enjoyed standing out, being different, following my own ways. Many memories of walking or spending time with my Japanese friends in San Francisco area, recalled the hostile stares, the occasional insults shouted from a passing car, slogans painted on the walls near Golden Gate Park and Japantown. I had learned to largely ignore these incidents. In Tokyo, I had railed against the mirror image mindset, in the bars of Manila, I had found myself breaking up fight after fight. And that's just the thing, when you try to be a friend to all, adversaries may see you as in league with their enemies. For the captives here on this filthy beach, the stakes had gotten very high, and in the midst of this horror, I was a ubiquitous participant in every alarming event.

Scapegoating is a major pastime of a population preoccupied with its own misery. In a prison or a POW camp situation any individual who is removed from the general population for any length of time has gained the suspicion of all who have been left behind to speculate. In such a situation as this, where so many privations and assaults had no apparent motive or logic, how easy it would be to focus on a scapegoat to make order of it all.

Thousands were in this situation, and outside of a few headquarters personnel and scattered individuals, numbering perhaps 50, if that many, no one knew me personally, knew my character. I was a nobody: a desk clerk. Here I was then, within 72 hours of capture, speaking fluent Japanese, appearing at each event of rising hostility, bowing politely to the guards, wearing an armband with Japanese characters, seeming to have such exceptional rapport with them that I could actually hold small talk and compliment them on their families, while an unfortunate captive's fate hung in the balance. And when I was successful in ending the danger, the suspicious could make note of the influence I seemed to have with their otherwise intransigent and cruel captors.

Worse, and perhaps most damning of all of the accusations that would be one day hurled at me, was that I would chant a Buddhist chant in Japanese over the bodies of the dead... which I did, of course. "Heathen chants" they would be called, and evidence of something despicable: In the ten years that followed those horrible and chaotic days, rumor and suspicion would be nurtured and embellished, so that by the time these tales were told, vague rumor would become vivid testimony, and dark suspicion would become glaring accusation.

Little by little the captives were allowed more freedom of movement. We were allowed to go to the periphery of the concentration camp area to relieve our bowels, and finally allowed to dig some slit trenches for latrines. The Japanese began to bring in scant supplies and some water, barely enough to sustain life. Many people were comatose and beyond saving. Some of the medical personnel got together an area that they called a sick bay, but there was little that could be done without supplies or even drinking water.

I found my commanding officer, Colonel Menzies, where he lay in a coma on the beach, and I had to do something about it. Up until this point I had dealt only with what situations had been thrust upon me, but the sight of my dying Colonel moved me to take a more assertive step. I went over to the remains of the hangar where the guards had set up a temporary shelter. When I got there, I could see that many of the Japanese soldiers were lying on the ground in various stages of delirium from the malaria they had contacted on Bataan. They had no quinine to treat it.

The guard commander was drunk, and I was able to talk him into allowing us to take ten of the worst cases among the captives up to the hospital in Malinta Tunnel. He gave me a written pass that allowed us to take a stretcher party bearing ten each day. Picking ten out of the 200 or so critical cases was done by taking the first ten we came to. In the first stretcher party, we carried Colonel Menzies. He did survive, and survived the war, and lived to speak in my defense years later.

I accompanied the stretcher party each day up to the hospital and returning we would carry whatever hospital supplies could be spared back down to the concentration camp area. Captives were being organized into work details. Bodies of the dead, Japanese, American and Filipino, littered the slopes and many work parties were required to carry them to a central location for cremation. Bodies of Japanese were taken first, gathered in handcarts, brought in, carefully stacked in piles and ceremoniously burned. Their ashes were swept up into individual boxes, boxes like those I had seen unloaded from the ships in Yokohama harbor just one year before. Only after all the Japanese bodies had been cremated, were the work details ordered to bring in the corpses of the defenders, which by then, a week after they had fallen, were bloated, blackened and rotting in the tropical sun. They were burnt in great piles and their ashes left to scatter in the wind.

Some work details were put to work restoring some of the least destroyed buildings, others were used to offload supplies being brought in from Manila, some were carrying and loading what spoils of war the Japanese were able to salvage from Corregidor. Some, like me, would be assigned to do KP work for the various guard details around the island. Refusal to participate in any of these work details meant death on the spot.

One day, when the stretcher party and I were about to return to the concentration camp area, the guard commander at the tunnel ordered me to remain behind. I was put into a small lateral tunnel directly behind the guard post with some other captives. We had been chosen to build the guards' cooking fires and wash their pots and pans and do whatever chores and errands asked of them.

This was occurring a week after our capture, and things were unpredictable from hour to hour. In terms of the formal surrender proceedings which were conducted in Manila, during this period those of us held on Corregidor were hostages, and would remain so until all Allied Forces in the Philippines laid down their weapons and joined the surrender; only then would they be considered prisoners of war. That day was not to arrive until June 9.

As battlefield captives we were subject to the orders of any Japanese soldier, of whatever rank; we were subject to interrogation and torture; in fact we were all subject to summary execution for any real or imagined offense, or attempt to escape, or for offering any resistance at all. Many were killed for simply not realizing the position we were in, and displaying the smallest amount of antagonism. The Japanese were extremely angry and nervous about their own position, and remained hostile about the horrendous battles they had had to fight to capture Bataan and Corregidor.

I was beginning to realize that my unique role could be expanded and to believe that the responsibility for the well being of my comrades was in my hands. My efforts were working, and I had saved many from the bayonet and saber. I had even been able, if time and circumstances allowed, to let the guard know that I was a Buddhist priest, and to risk a mild reproach of the guard's brutality. That had worked, too. If only I could make that facet more obvious to the Japanese, my effectiveness would be greatly enhanced. I found in one of the tunnel laterals a sort of hospital garment that I could wear in a way reminiscent of a priest's robe, and I began to make more overt displays of worship. I set up a makeshift shrine in the tunnel lateral where I was kept, and I would chant regularly each morning and evening; and especially loudly if there were some high-ranking Japanese officers inside the tunnel complex.

I had little reason to expect that I would survive the war, let alone to imagine that I would have to answer to my own government for this bizarre behavior.

I was quartered in a lateral near the interior entrance to the hospital tunnel, and I was often called in to interpret for the medical staff. Those who had been inside of the hospital since the capture were not as aware of their precarious status as were those who had been in the beach concentration camp. Those who were aware, like myself, were terribly concerned that the nurses might be raped, as they had been in Hong Kong and Singapore. An American woman had been raped after the fall of Bataan, just two miles away. Often, incidents had arisen when soldiers not on authorized patrol entered the hospital, looting and terrorizing the nurses. In my position near the hospital entrance these events would unfold right around the corner from me.

Colonel Cooper, the officer in charge of the hospital asked if I could intercede. It was extremely awkward to be making any request of the Japanese but I was emboldened by my success in creating the stretcher parties, appealed to the guard commander to stop the soldiers' intrusions. This was successful and the Japanese officer did put up a sign on a folding screen to the effect that the hospital was off limits to soldiers not on guard duty. I was feeling increasingly responsible for the welfare of all the captives. No one, I felt, was in a better position to improve conditions and prevent disaster. They were at all times in danger of massacre. Thankfully, none were raped on Corregidor.

One day the Japanese allowed the doctors and nurses out of the hospital tunnel and into another part of the tunnel complex in order to pick out some fresh clothes from the remaining supplies. As the medical personnel moved along the tunnel among the Japanese guards, they were talking and laughing and the nurses were acting flirtatiously toward the doctors. I knew how casual this was in our former context, I had been no prude in my own experience, believe me, but I also knew the standards of the Japanese culture. Fearing that the Japanese soldiers would interpret this light-hearted banter and posing as looseness and arouse them to consider rape. I had to make it clear to them that they had better tone down their behavior in front of the soldiers; and while I was on the subject, I told them not to go out the tunnel entrance for their romantic tete-a-tetes because they were in full view of many soldiers there as well. The medical personnel went along with my chaperoning begrudgingly, not realizing the danger they were in. There still was life going on inside the tunnels, social life even. Outside, conditions continued to be desperate.

In time, the captives became more aware of what was expected of them, of what were the limits of their freedom and most important, how to assess the mood of an individual guard confronting them. Failure on this last point could easily prove fatal. I had some advantage in this, as I had known many, many Japanese people in my childhood, had studied their history and culture, and so had many insights into their general psychology.

Part of the trouble we were having was that to the Japanese soldier, surrender was despicable; the Japanese soldier was expected to fight to the death no matter what, and if he could no longer fight, he was expected to commit suicide before allowing himself to fall into the hands of an enemy. Thus, as surrendered forces, we were beneath any respect and had no claim to human dignity or any right to compassion.

I was at the same time becoming increasingly aware of the light in which my fellow captives were seeing me. The few who knew me well, when we happened to come in contact would tell me, "John, do you know what they're saying about you?" My small circle of friends, of course, knew the rumors couldn't be true, but they were a miniscule percentage of the thousands of captives. I became aware of the stories, but there was no way I could counter them. I began to feel the hateful glares of those who saw me. There was no way I could acquit myself.

From time to time, in the weeks after its capture, Corregidor was visited by some higher ranking Japanese officers, who would come for a short while, look around and then leave. On one occasion, it became clear that someone very important was coming. The Japanese were in a heightened state of anticipation, and special preparations were being made. They had rigged up a canvas canopy part way up Malinta Hill and had placed a number of tables and chairs under it. I was ordered to take a tray of glasses filled with ice water up to this canopy but before I could get there, the dignitary had already arrived. He was Field Marshal Terauchi, a count in the Japanese nobility, an imposing figure, very tall for a Japanese and wearing white gloves. By the actions of the other Japanese around him, he obviously outranked them all. He was there to survey the captured territories and would report directly to the emperor.

This day, I pushed my luck to the extreme, in many ways and made a gamble that I shouldn't have survived. As I approached the canopied area, it was indicated that I should put the ice water down on a table very near to where the Field

Marshal was standing. As I did, I picked up one glass and bowing deeply, handed it to Terauchi. At this, perhaps suspecting poison, or at least a serious breach of etiquette, the Japanese aides bristled and moved to stop me. Instead Terauchi stopped them. Looking me directly in the eye, he took the glass and drank it. Bowing deeply again, I began to speak, in the classic dialect of an educated Japanese, in extremely polite yet reproachful tones, "I cannot believe it is justifiable." and pointing down to the concentration camp, "that there is practically no food and no water, does the emperor know of this?" One Japanese officer began to withdraw his sword. Count Terauchi gestured to him, without looking, to put it back, he turned to another aide and said, "See to it!" I bowed and hurried down the hill.

The next day, after Marshal Terauchi had gone, the Japanese brought several barrels of water, and some sacks of rice to the concentration camp, and although the drums had formerly contained oil and the water was oily, it was desperately needed much appreciated. Those at the concentration camp of course, had no way of knowing that I had risked my life for it, literally stuck out my neck for it; to the contrary, from what could be seen by those on the beach, there was that Sergeant Provoo bootlicking and kowtowing before the Japanese dignitary, and new damning rumors were spread among them.

It was in this atmosphere that a most tragic event occurred. I was sent one day by the guard commander into the hospital mess to simply get some water glasses. The mess officer was veterinary Captain Burton C. Thomson. When I asked for the glasses, the captain responded angrily that they were short of everything and that he couldn't spare anything for the Japs, and ordered me to get out. I didn't know what to do. I realized the danger to Captain Thomson, though he did not. Instead of returning to the guard commander, I went back to the chore I had been doing before. Soon, however, the guard commander came over to me and demanded to know where the glasses were. I said that he could not get them. The guard commander said "Why not?" and I replied, "The officer in charge will not let them leave the hospital." Two guards were sent into the hospital to get Captain Thomson, and soon returned with him. The guard commander asked Captain Thomson in English for the items he wanted, to which the captain replied that he needed all the supplies that were in the hospital. The Guard commander flew into a rage..."No one can disobey the order of a Japanese officer. Everything here belongs to the Emperor, your lives belong to the Emperor!" He told the guards to take the Captain below to the concentration camp area. That was the last we saw of him and though there were rumors, we never knew what had happened to him until after the war. According to court testimony given ten years later, Captain Thomson was taken to a small metal building near the concentration camp and interrogated for about forty-five minutes. From there he was taken to Monkey Point, tied to a bush and executed.

Rumors of all kinds run rampant through a prison camp, but when rumors reached me that Captain Thomson had been executed at Monkey Point, I felt an intense dread that it might be true. I went to the guard commander and asked what had become of Captain Thomson. He told me to shut up and not ask about it again, which tended to confirm my worst fear. I began to suffer terribly, and could not get it out of my mind. With all that I had been able to accomplish with my intercessions, I had not been able to save Captain Thomson.

My conscience offered me a hundred ways I could have handled the situation differently; what I could have said, or should have said, but I knew it was too late ...Captain Thomson was dead... and I would certainly be damned for it.

After this, suspicions became established fact in the minds of many of the captive population, and the hostility toward me more overt. Colonel Cooper ordered me not to come into the hospital area again, but not long after that I was called into Col. Cooper's office. There were a number of members of the hospital staff, Col. Cooper and a Japanese medical officer who spoke English. When I entered the room, Col. Cooper looked at the floor, the others looked away and the Japanese officer glowered at me and began to pull out his sword. Col. Cooper said, "Oh no, no. Not here. This is a hospital." I was sent back out. Apparently those in the room had used the incident of the nurses' flirtatiousness to convince the Japanese officer that I had been overbearing and claiming some authority in telling them to subdue their behavior.

I was at my wit's end; isolated in my despair. The nervous energy that had kept me going these awful weeks now failed me and I came down with a serious case of dysentery. I was taken to the hospital, where I was anything but welcome. I had at least one friend in the hospital, Captain Heimbach, and that saved my life. It was an attempted murder. One medical officer had given me a lethal injection under the guise of treatment for dysentery, and Captain Heimbach, finding me with virtually no vital signs, was able to revive me with some kind of counteracting shot. Captain Heimbach survived the war, and testified in my defense years later.

Beginning in the 1st week of May, captives from the concentration camp were taken down to the North Mine docks and crammed aboard ships and taken to Manila. On June 9 the Japanese accepted formally the surrender of Wainwright's command, the entire Philippines. The battle captives were now prisoners of war, which in reality meant no change in conditions. The prisoners were given numbers, which were painted on the backs of the shirts they were captured in, and also numbered in groups of ten. If any of one's group of ten tried to escape, all ten would be executed. General Wainwright's position was worse. If any of the thousands under his command escaped, he would be executed. Wainwright was quoted as saying "If any of you take a notion to escape, let me know, I'm going with you".

Finally the day came when the hospital tunnels were evacuated, and all the patients and staff were taken off the island. As the island and the tunnels grew less and less inhabited, I grew increasingly afraid. At last I was removed from the tunnel and sent up to the remains of Topside barracks where I was housed with a larger group of prisoners, about 200. We were divided into work details, which were sent out each day to perform various tasks of cleaning up the island; gathering abandoned weapons, clearing unexploded ordnance, and removing the large chunks of concrete and other rubble that littered the roadways.

The prisoners at Topside were allowed to establish our own mess, and those who worked daily at the North Mine docks unloading and loading the boats from Manila brought back whatever bags of red rice and fresh fruit the Filipino workers had been able to smuggle in.

Things were slightly better here, there were fewer guards and I wasn't as closely watched. I was relieved to be among a larger group of prisoners. The most ugly and potentially lethal web of suspicion had left with the hospital staff. I was able to collect myself and regain some of my sanity.

I was a kid through all this, most of us were. August 6, 1942 was my 25th birthday, and conditions actually allowed for a celebration of sorts. Adam Sabotka, the cook, was even able to get together the ingredients for a cake, frosted with shaving cream, which was scraped off, of course, before being eaten. It was a few days in which I could forget that ahead of us lay at least years of hunger and imprisonment before the war could be over. In such a situation, one does not realistically look into the future, so little of it is predictable or in one's control. One does his best to survive the ordeal of this day, and get something to eat. Both Adam Sabotka and I survived the war and met again, years later in Baltimore, Maryland, and recalled the day when a piece of birthday cake represented a miracle, and the best meal we would have in three years of captivity.

*   *   *   *   *

Iva could not board her ship on December 2, 1941, because she had no passport. When the war began a few days later, Iva was stranded in an environment that was increasingly hostile to her. Agents of the domestic security police called at the home of her Aunt and Uncle, pressuring her to accept Japanese citizenship. She repeatedly refused. She tried to get herself repatriated through the Red Cross as did other Americans, but still her lack of a passport prevented her leaving.

Her Aunt and Uncle were beginning to receive official and unofficial harassment for having an enemy alien under their roof, so she moved out to spare them further difficulty. She began to do odd jobs of English language typing at the culture school she had been attending and to give her teacher's children piano lessons.

Finally in June 1942 she managed to get a job as a part time English language typist for the Domei News Agency, typing transcripts of English language radio broadcasts so that others on the staff could translate them into Japanese. The security police continued to pressure her into changing her citizenship, but she steadfastly refused.

In August she was finally accepted for repatriation aboard a Red Cross ship, but by this time she no longer had the money for her passage. It was her last chance to get out.

She began to make a life for herself there, and became fond of Felipe D'Aquino, a Portuguese/Japanese fellow employee of the Domei News Agency who also had foreign citizenship and was definitely pro-American. They eventually married in April 1945.

In August of 1943, Iva got another job as an English language typist...at the studios of Radio Tokyo, not knowing that this was the threshold of the Japanese military's psychological warfare section.

Nichijo

Chapter Eight

College of Hard Knocks

In the middle of August, the remaining prisoners on Corregidor were taken down to the North Mine docks and loaded aboard tugs and taken to Manila. We were disembarked at the foot of Dewey Boulevard and marched through the city's streets. Starved, sick, ragged and emaciated, we made such a pathetic sight that we were not taken by the shortest route, but several extra miles, so that we would pass through the most crowded parts of the city. This was to give our degradation the maximum exposure before the Filipino population.

Manila was a much different place than it was when I was here six months before. There had been some aerial bombings, even though the city had been declared open and militarily abandoned. For the most part, it was physically intact. The Japanese occupying forces with trucks and tanks and artillery moved through the city. Japanese troops fresh from their bloody victories marched in columns. Japanese propaganda operatives drove through the streets with loudspeakers on the tops of their vehicles. "Greater East Asia Co-prosperity Sphere", was the primary vision. The idea being that Japan was liberating Asians from their American and European colonial masters. Their slogan, "Asia for the Asians" blared from every possible public address system was being force-fed to the populace. The people were not accepting this clumsy façade by any means. The Filipinos lining the way of our route encouraged us with smiles and furtive "V" victory signs with their fingers.

We passed through the walls of the old city and finally reached the ancient Spanish prison, Bilibid Prison. The prison had been used as a staging area and distribution point for prisoners coming from Corregidor. They had been kept there a short while and then moved out to other locations. Many thousands had been paraded through Manila before our group. There remained at Bilibid over 2000 prisoners.

My reputation had preceded me, but fortunately, the first person I met had some insight into my situation. The American who had been placed in charge of POW's at Bilibid was Naval Warrant Officer Goodman; he spoke to me first: "I've heard a lot of things about you, some of them very good and some very bad. I like to form my own opinions, so we'll just take it from here." It soon became clear why Mr. Goodman was so understanding. He could speak Japanese pretty well and he had been thrust into a role similar role to mine, and suffered some of the same suspicions, though not as extreme.

I watched as Goodman went through his paces. Approaching the guard commander, he bowed deeply and began to converse with him in polite and amicable tones. Soon he turned to the group of new arrivals, carrying out the guard's instructions. He assigned the new arrivals to low, temporary wooden structures within the high-walled compound. As I watched him carry out the duties of his situation with the same constraints and cultural sensibilities that I had, I could see clearly how westerners would misconstrue it. He really had no choice if he were to serve the needs of his fellow prisoners. Of course, of course, he had to act that way. And so had I. This time someone else had that thankless job.

Bilibid prison is right in the midst of Manila's city streets. Its high walls and the open ground around them made it necessary for Filipinos to expose themselves dangerously to help us. They would risk their lives daily to throw hard-boiled eggs and fruit over the walls with the guards shooting at them. Still, it was not enough. What I most remember about Bilibid was hunger and literal starvation, and these brave and desperate attempts by the Filipinos to keep us alive.

The dirt floor of the open-air compound had been used as a graveyard for the many who had died there, and were still dying there. When the rains came and the compound flooded, decayed limbs of the dead reached up from beneath the ground. The hells I have witnessed on this earth.

There at Bilibid prison, again I met Captain Wallace Ince. Ince had spent most of the six months of war in the Navy tunnel section of the Malinta Tunnel complex on Corregidor. I did not see him during this time, but we could hear him, of course, on the radio. The Navy Tunnel was the location of the large short wave radio transmitters used for military communications as well as news and entertainment programs for the Allied troops in the field. Ince, having been a top civilian announcer in Manila, was put in charge of the news and music program, "The Voice of Freedom."

When Corregidor was captured, Ince was of special interest to the Japanese; they wanted to use him for propaganda purposes, if possible. He had been held for interrogation and kept under close confinement for months, and questioned at great length. He had fallen under the suspicion of his fellow prisoners, as any who seemed to be of particular value to the captors and had often been quartered separate from the others. He sat alone when I arrived, shunned by the rest.

I, of course, was not impressed by the suspicions of others. Ince was glad to have someone to talk to and had something special to relate to me. He was going on a secret mission, he said, to Tokyo. He wouldn't say anything more about it or why he had told me. I had no reason to think it would involve me. Captain Ince was soon gone from Bilibid, and I didn't think about it much more. In about October 1942, about a month later, Wallace Ince and young Norman Reyes arrived in Tokyo to begin this "secret mission".

Norman Reyes was a Philippine national on Ince's staff, doing some of the broadcasting. It was Reyes who had the sad duty to broadcast the news that Bataan had fallen to the enemy. Reyes was barely nineteen, fifteen years younger than Ince and excited to be getting this valuable experience in broadcast. It was a rare opportunity for a Philippine teenager.

When Ince and Reyes fell into the hands of the Japanese, they had already been viewed as having unique wartime skills as propaganda broadcasters, and the Japanese were eager to bend these skills to their own war effort. Ince and Reyes were taken to Manila as soon as they were identified and placed in the dungeon at Fort Santiago, the Old Spanish fortress. They were exhaustively interrogated as to their potential. Young Reyes could be forced to cooperate, and when it was discovered that Ince had a Philippine wife and two small children, the Japanese knew that it would not be difficult to gain his compliance also. It was arranged that Ince and Reyes would be taken to Tokyo at the earliest possible opportunity.

Early in September, I was taken out of Bilibid with most of the other prisoners and paraded again through the streets of Manila to the docks and loaded aboard ships. They were troop transport ships, and below decks had been arranged into wooden platforms about four feet apart. Prisoners were jammed in far beyond capacity and the hatch covers were put in place and battened down. It may have been days that the ships lay there at dockside and it got hotter and hotter inside the holds. The air was foul and putrid and the bilge sloshed with their sewage. We were nearly suffocating and men were dying and there was no way to get the bodies out. Many lost their minds in there. That's another of the hells I have endured on this Earth.

At last we could hear the engines start up and we felt ourselves moving away from the dock. After several hours, the hatches were opened. Prisoners were ordered up on deck. We were outside of Manila Bay but still within the sight of land. The fresh air revived the survivors and our dead were thrown overboard. It was a clear day and the Philippines were disappearing in the distance to the south. We were in a convoy of several other troop ships and freighters and some destroyer escorts. The convoy moved in an erratic course apparently to avoid Allied submarines. We were being taken to Taiwan 500 miles North of Manila.

The convoy arrived at Takao, a small harbor on the

southwest coast of Taiwan, and surviving prisoners were herded off the many cramped troop ships and onto the docks. Scarcely had we disembarked when a squadron of American planes appeared overhead and swooped in for a strafing attack not knowing who we were, below on this Japanese naval base. We dove for whatever cover we could find. I found myself on a wooden catwalk just below the heavy planking of the dock. Many of us huddled there until the strafing was over and the Japanese ordered us back onto the dock.

All prisoners were sprayed with a strong smelling disinfectant under our armpits and around our genitals. A medical team inserted a glass rod in the rectum of each man and prepared a culture to check for various ailments and parasites, particularly amoebic dysentery.

Then we were marched through the streets of Takao to the train station. The inhabitants' reaction was much different than in Manila. The Japanese had ruled the island since 1895, and most descendants of the aborigines and Chinese immigrants had grown up under the Japanese administration, and had no particular affinity for the American captives. This fact, made the possibility of escape rather remote since there would be no anti-Japanese underground to assist and hide escapees as in the Philippines.

We arrived at the train station, were put on board passenger cars, crowded but not terribly so, and blindfolded so that we would not be able to survey military installations along our route to Karenko, on the Eastern Coast of the Island of Taiwan.

Outwardly, Karenko was a beautiful place. On the coast only a few miles from the base of almost sheer mountains rising to 10,000 feet. The grounds had a neat, well-maintained appearance and at first glance it seemed that the prisoners' lot would be better here. It was in some respects and it wasn't in others.

Captain Imamura, the camp's insipid commander, greeted the new arrivals as he had the Generals, including Wainwright, Beebe, Moore and others, several weeks before. We were called to attention, required to bow to the commander, and bow in the direction of the Imperial Palace, just as we would each morning for our entire stay there. Then Captain Imamura read his standard speech, made just barely intelligible by the camp's interpreter. The speech extolled the virtues of the "Greater East Asia Co-prosperity Sphere, the courage and sacrifice of the peace-loving Japanese people, and the wisdom and compassion of the Emperor, to whose mercy they owed their lives".

Following this preamble, the camp commander made four very strong points:

We would follow the orders of the guards, and our lives would be in danger if we did not.

We would be required to work, and we were not to complain about anything.

Our captors would not "tolerate any attitude of white man's superiority over yellow people".

We were required to bow as the commander left the field.

The guards ordered us to strip to our underwear, and we were issued undersized Japanese uniforms, which barely reached to our elbows and knees, but sadly, due to our prolonged malnutrition, could easily be closed at the waist. Most of us had had no shoes since Corregidor and we were issued awkward wooden clogs. We were assigned to barracks and issued our first meal; a handful of insect infected rice, and some very watery "soup". Three times a day for the next eight months, this was our basic ration, clearly not enough to live on.

Combined with inadequate medical care, this was a diet on which to waste away and die. It took a definite act of will, a commitment to survival to stay alive. Those of us who let ourselves slide into despair died in a short time, and even many of the strong-willed, through a compounding of disease and malnutrition could not sustain themselves.

What it took to survive was an indefatigable will to resist our tormentors and find ways to supplement our diet. It took the willingness to eat snails and grasshoppers, to regard the worms and weevils in our rice as a palatable source of additional protein, to value an occasional papaya leaf as a source of vitamins and enzymes when added to our soup, to experiment with eating the bark of trees to find some small measure of added nutrients. Food is the constant preoccupation of those hovering near starvation; it fills the thoughts of every waking moment and haunts their dreams. Prisoners' diaries characteristically contain elaborate recipes, imaginary feasts, recollections of great restaurants and orgiastic banquets of their pasts. Any day that brought an additional morsel of food was recorded as a memorable occasion.

Still, we watched ourselves and each other literally waste away; watched our skin sag and our skeletons protrude. Hunger made us extremely irritable, often toward each other. Hunger made us sensitive to the smallest discrepancy in the portioning out of our daily "meals". Hunger made many among us give in to despair and thereby fall victim to the myriad of diseases that we all hosted to varying degrees.

I was never one to let my spirit be beaten. It tore at me and disgusted me to see so many of my fellows quit. I recognized the psychological and physical danger of this inner surrender. I recognized the imperative to stay involved in something positive, anything that could occupy the intellect and keep up the morale of one's self and those around him.

The great paradox of life as a prisoner of war on Taiwan was that it offered what can be described as a truly pure academic life for those willing to grasp it. There were a number of very high ranking British and Dutch officers as well as high civilian officials from Hong Kong and Singapore that were being held at Karenko and some had managed to bring along complete sets of volumes of British history. There was even a Victrola and a collection of classical records. British officers formed informal lectures on military history, strategy and tactics. Anyone who had any great knowledge in a particular field would make himself available for the enlightenment of others. I did what I could to coach those interested in Japanese language, a most useful tool in our present circumstances.

Everyone, of course, quickly became aware of the

meaning of a small number of Japanese commands. Each morning the prisoners were assembled on the parade ground and called to attention; "Kioski!" We were ordered to bow toward the Imperial Palace; "Kirei!" and to count off; "Bango!" We had all learned to count in Japanese. Then we were sent off to our various work details. All prisoners of whatever rank were put to work; maintaining the grounds, working in the small garden, cleaning the guards' cooking pots, and even General Wainwright was put to work herding goats.

For a short while, we were subjected to only occasional slappings by the guards. But in early October word reached the camp that the Japanese civilians who were repatriated from Australia and the U.S. had been mistreated and their property confiscated. The guards were determined to retaliate by mistreating those at hand. Slappings turned into ugly indiscriminate beatings, some quite brutal and severe. Any slightest infraction of the camp's rules would bring a blow from the flat of a bayonet or rifle butt. Many required hospitalization including General Wainwright who was beaten until he dropped for exiting the latrine through the wrong door and once was gashed on the wrist by a bayonet during a beating.

Most of the prisoners had dysentery and diarrhea, which meant having to get up and go out to the latrine at least once during the night. There was always a POW monitor at the door of the barracks to mark off the time and the name of the prisoner going out and coming back in. Stepping from the porch we would always encounter a guard, either standing in sight, or behind a large bush there. When he hid behind the bush, one could choose to bow or not bow, it made little difference. If there was no bow he would jump out and hit the you for not bowing; if you bowed when he was hidden, the guard would jump out and hit you for bowing to the bush. This became so routine that we expected to be hit when we got up in the night and you learned to roll with the punch, so that it hardly got you awake.

My status at this camp was just one of the lower ranking POW's amongst many, which I much preferred to the spotlight of suspicion I had been placed in on Corregidor. The situation was stable compared to the horrible uncertainty of our captive state just after surrender. We weren't in as close contact with the guards and we knew more or less what to expect. Though I was occasionally assigned as squad leader on a rotating basis, I was usually a face in the crowd, which I much preferred. I wasn't called upon to intercede in violent confrontations or to interpret the guards' orders and thus I was free from being the focus of rumors that I had been.

Even when a most suspicious incident occurred, my fellows were able to see it for what it was. At Karenko, POW's were not constantly under close watch by the guards, but when anyone in military uniform entered the compound, the first of us to see him was required to call the others to attention and all bow deeply. One day I was standing near the barracks at the time of the changing of the guard, and a new group of guards came across the compound and, of course, everyone bowed. As I stood back up straight from my bow I was shocked to see one of the Japanese soldiers leave the group and come rushing toward me. The guard, instead of hitting me, grabbed me, hugged me and began talking excitedly in English. This was Robert Yamanaka; he had been a friend of mine at Commerce High School in San Francisco, we had even attended the same Buddhist Temple. Robert had moved to Japan long before the

119

war.

We were able to have many conversations during the course of my time at Karenko, and we even debated the outcome of the war, a topic that would have normally been disastrous between guard and prisoner. Still, we were each loyal to opposing sides and finally my insistence that the Americans would win ended such discussions. We were able, in small ways, to ameliorate conditions for some of the worst medical cases. Later on, when the entire camp was moved to Shirakawa, another location on Taiwan, Robert was made camp interpreter and as such was present at some interrogations in which some British officers were given rather severe beatings. At Shirakawa, our relationship was quite distant.

One day while still at Karenko, it was announced that a Red Cross team was coming and a POW delegation was appointed to greet them, with the admonition from the Japanese "Remember, we'll be here after they are gone." A "store" was hastily constructed but it was more like a Hollywood set. They had a number of bottles of sweet syrup and soy sauce and even some oranges and tangerines that were supposedly for sale. The "store" and its inventory lasted only a few days beyond the Red Cross visit. The Red Cross representatives were Axis Italians and of little benefit to the prisoners of war, and after taking pictures of us making our play-acted purchases, they left.

The POW officers were given a monthly allowance in yen, and since there was nothing to buy with it, the Japanese officers talked them into putting up the money to buy and raise some pigs. Quite a few pigs were raised but only a few were actually eaten by the POW's, these on occasional days when a Japanese inspecting officer came by to check on conditions. Sometimes we were able to save a pig's blood from the slaughtering, for a little extra nutrition, but for the most part the pig enterprise only allowed us to supplement our diets with what pig food we were able to steal.

I was perhaps the only one in that camp that was given a real chance to escape from this scene of starvation and brutality. There arrived at the camp one day two Japanese civilians and they called a few prisoners to be interviewed. I was one of those to be called. Apparently when my story about being a Buddhist priest was checked out through Tokyo, the Buddhist authorities of the Nichirenshu at Minobu had discovered I was a prisoner of war. Since that time they had been doing what they could to intercede. The Japanese civilians offered me the opportunity to return to Minobu and continue my training for the priesthood. I could return to Minobu, the misty and serene culmination of my childhood dreams. It was a chance to escape this life of cruel oppression and to return to the life that was of my own choosing. I would be fed, clothed and nurtured again in an atmosphere of wisdom and compassion.

There was no real choice in my mind. I didn't hesitate to say no. My place was with my fellow prisoners, I couldn't leave them and abandon my oath of allegiance to the Army. In spite of what my military service had been, I loved the Army. The many fine officers I had met at Karenko inspired me. I admired their devotion to duty in the face of the most humiliating and debasing circumstances. It was my opportunity to demonstrate to myself that I was worthy of being in their company and receiving their tutelage. I had to say no. I was now a sergeant in the U.S. Army, and my loyalties were to my fellow enlisted men, my commanding officers and my country.

Minobu would still be there if I survived the war. Minobu would shimmer in my dreams and the face of my Lord Abbot, my master, would beckon, but awake I felt more strongly about Colonel Menzies and General Wainwright and the many friends I had found amidst starvation and brutality. It was a decision I never regretted during the final years of the war. It wasn't until my own government turned against me after liberation, that I would ever even doubt that I had done the right thing. Even so, it was the right thing.

It might have been different had we not found ways to deal with our torment. We found ways to strengthen our morale; to continue resisting the Japanese in whatever small ways we could; ways to occupy ourselves and entertain each other; to help the sick; to educate each other; to remain civilized while being treated worse than animals.

The Japanese did not allow us to listen to the radio or to read newspapers, but we did find ways to monitor the progress of the war. On rare occasions we were able to get a forbidden copy of a Japanese newspaper and translate its pronouncements into English and then read between the lines. I was able to add to this intelligence by engaging my old school chum, Robert Yamanaka, in debate about the outcome of the war; invariably, Robert would brag about victory after victory, and how the Imperial Navy had sunk the American fleet again. It was obvious that each time the Japanese had one of their "victories" that the location was considerably closer to the Japanese homeland.

We learned to maintain our dignity and self-esteem while

being beaten, abused and humiliated; we learned not to show the pain being inflicted. We would gather together to sing or listen to record concerts. As Christmas of 1942 approached we made crude gifts for each other and even managed to put together a Christmas variety show: Christmas carols, comedy skits, a magic act, and General Wainwright appropriately reciting "General Gas 'n Oil", a comic ballad of an old horse cavalry officer confronting the new modern "cavalry"...mechanized tanks.

We did find ways to survive, physically and psychologically, but as winter came on, our health problems were magnified. The air in our unheated barracks grew colder and colder. In our lightweight uniforms we became cold and we stayed cold for months. Our bodies had been acclimatized to the tropical heat. Now in our emaciated condition even the subtropical Taiwan winter seemed bone chilling.

One day in January, the Japanese passed out questionnaires to all prisoners, which required us to list our hobbies, interests and occupations before the war. At that particular moment, it was my turn as squad leader. I asked my nearest superior officer, my good friend and mentor Colonel Enos how we should respond. Colonel Enos asked General Wainwright, and the answer passed back down the line was that there didn't seem to be any reason not to fill them out truthfully.

The questionnaire seemed especially interested in musical and theatrical experience. There was speculation among the prisoners that the Japanese were forming a POW variety show to boost morale in the camps. They weren't. I filled the questionnaire out like the others, truthfully, but omitting anything of military significance. I wrote that I had had theatrical and radio experience in San Francisco before the war. This resume brought me a world of trouble. I should have put basket weaving. The questionnaires were turned in and forgotten.

There are two types of beri-beri and by the end of February 1943 nearly everybody had one or the other. The disease is caused by malnutrition and particularly the deficiency of Vitamin B. One of its effects is the loss of control over the muscles of the toes, which gives one a characteristic "slapfoot" walk. General Wainwright had the less severe dry form marked by flaking skin on the shins and massive "dandruff". Wet beri-beri makes the lower extremities and testicles swell up to grotesque proportions. The disease can be prevented or cured by eating rice or grains with the shells still on the kernels; unmilled grains contain Vitamin B. The only food provided was polished rice. What little Vitamin B we got, if any, was in the stolen pig food.

At the end of February Colonel Bunker's body had swollen to twice its normal size from wet beri-beri. Near his death he could not recognize his oldest friends, not even General Wainwright, when they came to pay their respects. Funerals had been a regular event at Karenko as they were at all POW camps, but now their number was increasing. Everyone had a complex of diseases and dietary deficiencies that could make them the next. Each of us made out our wills, not in despair, but in realistically confronting our condition. Just one series of misfortunes or a simple cold could put one over the edge beyond recovery. I awoke one morning to find that the man in the bunk next to me, my good friend Sergeant Cavenaugh, had died during the night. Nearly starved like the rest of us, he contracted strep throat for two days and the drain on his vital forces had been too great.

I had the wet form of beri-beri. My legs and ankles were swollen and covered with running sores that would not heal. My teeth were painfully abscessed and rotting and I had to borrow pliers from the man who made our wooden clogs and pulled them myself. I did survive.

In April 1943, some of the highest-ranking officers including General Wainwright were moved to another camp on Taiwan as a prelude to being taken to Manchuria for the duration. American successes in the Pacific made it necessary to move POW's from the coastline. In May, the rest of the camp was moved to another camp at Shirakawa, on the other side of the island high on the vast westward sloping alluvial plain.

I stayed at this camp for about five months. Everything was better here: the weather warmer, the indiscriminate and severe beatings had eased up after Christmas, and now it was mainly occasional slappings or a prod with bayonet or rifle butt, when working too slowly in the fields. Prisoners of war throughout the Far East were put into work gangs: as longshoremen on the Yokohama docks, as yardmen in the Osaka Railway station, as machinists in Kobe factories, as miners in the coal pits at Kyushu, as expendable slaves in the construction of a jungle railway across Thailand to Burma. Here at Shirakawa it was spring, and POW's were set to work planting vast fields of sweet potatoes and peanuts. Our rations weren't improved but we could easily supplement our diets by surreptitiously eating what we were planting. We were put on a regular routine of work, our health improved and we began to believe we might see the end of our ordeal and survive the war after all. We would pass a reservoir each day on the way back from the fields and if the guards were in a good mood, we were allowed a brief swim. First, however, we had to beat the water with sticks to drive the poisonous snakes up to one end where they stayed just long enough for us to take a quick dip.

The days and months rolled on, they merged into one memory; of days in the fields, of nights among my friends, of scholarly lectures, of philosophical debates, the ignorant brutality of guards demonstrating inferiority while asserting their insecure superiority, the hunger, the never ending effort to find one more morsel of nutrition, the caring shown by hungry men bringing what little food we could find back to those too weak and sick to forage for themselves.

Life in prison camp is a voluminous history of small heroisms; risks taken for the smallest victory, whether it be a few extra morsels of burnt rice scraped from guards' cooking pots while doing their kitchen chores and smuggling it back as an extra ration for the older and sicker, or the passing of forbidden news of the war; a forbidden newspaper obtained, translated and its between the lines message deciphered and passed among the ragged soldiers, or a beating taken unflinchingly; or interceding in the beating of another knowing that likely the torment would be redirected to the rescuer; of using whatever special talents or insights one had arrived with to benefit the well-being and morale of his fellows.

My special contributions were neither greater nor smaller than others. Everyone did what he could. What I brought was knowledge of the language, the customs and the psychology of our captors. I also had a unique connection with Robert

Yamanaka, who was now the camp interpreter. Robert himself was in an awkward position. He was very much a loyal Japanese soldier, and had to participate in some rather ugly and brutal interrogations, but paradoxically, he was still my high school chum, a San Francisco boy who could not help but feel empathy for the imprisoned. He did what he could to alleviate conditions; to keep the seriously ill from going on work details, to let the prisoners know what was happening in a way the other guards could not. I was able to add to the general knowledge of the war situation by my debates with Robert, and to find out what was going to be tolerated and how harshly particular infractions were going to be dealt with.

The POW's, it must be said, were used by the Japanese to further their war effort. We did plant many, many acres of sweet potatoes and peanuts and we were kept there through the entire growing season and brought in the harvest. While the food added to the Imperial Army's larder, it added to our own sustenance as well, though it had to be gleaned secretly and smuggled back to camp.

When the harvest was in, it was me who brought the first news to the group via Robert Yamanaka, that the camp was going to be moved. The Japanese never gave the prisoners an overview of what was happening to us, but in retrospect, it was plain that our purpose at Shirakawa was to be farm hands. It was October now. The crop was in, and we were moving on to some other purpose for the winter.

There came a day, probably in October of 1943, when a fairly large group of prisoners, with me among them, were loaded aboard trucks and driven to another POW camp, at Tamazato, on the Eastern coast South of Karenko. We were placed in a large wire enclosure about one-quarter mile from the train station with a large number of Allied prisoners whom we hadn't met before.

It was apparently a time for a great shift in the locations of POW's in East Asia. The camp was being used as a staging ground for the sorting and transferring of prisoners from many locations in the Philippines and Southeast Asia. It was plain to the men from Shirakawa camp that ours had not been the worst lot suffered by Allied POW's. It had been our good fortune that we worked at an agricultural camp. Many prisoners from other camps were nearly mustard yellow and had the distended bellies and hollow eyes of the severely malnourished. The others had had more severe physical abuse and they spoke hauntedly of the fact that the routine murder of the weak or disobedient had never let up since those horrible days on Corregidor. Thousands had been literally worked to death. The fact that so many of us were being shipped north bespoke the fact of Allied military successes in the South, but there was little for us to rejoice in. We were the retreating army's hostages; it renewed the horror of our predicament.

Of my long years in prison camps, my days at Shirakawa were the least horrible. It even had its moments when my spirit and intellect could soar again, thanks to the truly fine caliber of my fellow prisoners. It was here, as I would often say in years to come, that I learned the true meaning of that military cliché, "Duty is a thing never done." It was here I gained an insight as to what it was to be a prisoner of war and still a soldier, to find ways to resist within while outwardly oppressed. It was the words of my mentors at Shirakawa that would grant me the perspective to deal with the ordeal that would soon confront me, to find ways to serve my country under close guard from the middle of the enemy camp.

Being a prisoner of war is not the end of resistance; it is a great test of the human will. Being disarmed, caged, starved and beaten does not eliminate resistance; it drives it within. The worst has happened; one's mortal enemy has gained control of all outward physical circumstances; even life and death is at the whim of the captor. They have the guns, they have the food, they control one's movements through every hour of every day, but the man within still owns himself and can commit himself to a greater cause. If there is any lesson in my story for those who find themselves in the position of national leaders who order people into war to be maimed, killed or captured it is this; we remain engaged in the conflict; capture is not the end for us. We never stopped resisting.

Nichijo

Chapter Nine

Radio Tokyo

Trucks were carrying prisoners to the docks at Tamazato; another convoy to somewhere was being formed. Again we were placed in the cramped hold of a Japanese troopship and locked in. It wasn't nearly as horrible as the trip from Manila, it wasn't nearly as hot and the convoy proceeded as soon as it was loaded, to the North.

A POW can see only his past and his present. You have no concept of what is being done with you, what the overall picture is, no more than live poultry on the way to market. You would rather not recount the recent past, and the horrors it contained; it might very well foretell the tenor of the future. You fine-tune the perceptions of the moment. On a November day in 1943, I was on a train pulling away from the dock on the coast of the main Japanese island of Honshu. We were headed for Tokyo. I looked out the window. The Japanese countryside looked similar to three years earlier when I had toured in robes in the company of my fellow novice priests. It did not yet bear the scars of American bombs but there was something different about it. It had to do mostly with the people's appearance and the ubiquitous military trucks and military uniforms. Gone were the kimonos. Women wore the baggy pantaloons called mompi. People had a characteristically distressed look, the faintly bleary-eyed look of those who had worked, and sacrificed and worried too long, without relief or reward. They were a population straining bleakly under burdens imposed, not shouldered willingly.

The train stopped somewhere between Yokohama and Tokyo. We were pushed from the train onto the railway station platforms, and into waiting trucks. We were moved through city streets to the coast again and over a manmade causeway, a wooden pier, onto an oval island within Tokyo Bay. The trucks were driven past the camp commander's headquarters and into a walled compound no bigger than a football field. It had a high bamboo fence with barbed wire at the top. Prisoners' quarters were in the center. This was Omori camp. "Tokyo POW Camp Omori-ku Iriarai Kila" was its full name, later on it was known as simply "Hell Camp". My stay there was short, and foreboding.

With the addition of the new arrivals, there were several thousand prisoners, quartered in unheated wooden barracks. It was freezing cold. In our lightweight synthetic fiber uniforms and our barefoot wooden clogs, that form of misery we experienced at Karenko had returned. The food was different, but not any better. We never had rice again once we reached Japan, but rather a combination of coarser grains, the dominant one being millet. It was best described as a gruel made from chicken feed, with some odds and ends of vegetables, mainly daikon radish, and on rare days we got a small issue of beans.

There were a great many prisoners there from the far flung theaters of war in which they had been captured. There was a large contingent of Dutch prisoners there along with their Indonesian comrades, a similarly large group of Australians, Malaysians and British, who had been captured in Singapore. We were housed together. Day by day, individuals were taken from the group and interrogated, as they would report upon returning, by Japanese civilians. The questions seemed to center around entertainment. There seemed to be, collected in Omori camp, most of the members of a British band, giving rise to a rumor that the Japanese were getting up a troupe of POW entertainers. It also became apparent that many of those assembled in the camp had done various forms of writing, or had radio or theatrical experience. This was, of course, the result of questionnaires like those we had filled out at Karenko nearly nine months before. Those interrogated could only surmise what was happening from the questions asked. The interrogators gave out no information.

When my turn came, I was summoned to a room at the front of the compound. It was not at all like a military tribunal, not like the life or death confrontations on Corregidor. It was less like a trial and more like a job interview. There were two Japanese in civilian clothes. They were mostly interested in my childhood experience in radio acting and I answered their questions truthfully, not realizing where it all was leading.

Some days after this meeting, at the morning formation of prisoners, a number of names were called out: Dutch, British and Americans, and mine. We were marched out of the compound and up in front of the Camp Commander's headquarters. The Commander came out with an interpreter and made a very brusque and ominous statement... "Whatever happens to you after you leave this camp, I am in no way responsible for." Once he was certain this was understood, he went back inside, and the guards prodded the seventeen of us onto waiting trucks, at bayonet-point. We were driven across the causeway and into the city of Tokyo.

In a short time, we reached our destination. It was formerly a school for foreigners that taught the language and culture of Japan, Nihongo Bunkwa Gakkou..."Japanese Culture School." It had been renamed, "Surugdai Technical Research Center" and taken over by the military for their own purposes. The courtyard in the rear of the three story main building had been converted into a prison camp compound and the long low two-story dormitory within had become POW barracks. To us it was known simply as " Bunkwa Camp".

We were unloaded from the trucks and nudged with rifle butts through the large archway that led under and through the four story main building into the courtyard behind. We were ordered to line up single file against the wall on one side of the courtyard. Two guards set up a machine gun pointed at us, fed a belt of bullets into it, cocked it and removed the safety catch. A scar faced Japanese officer strode to the center of the courtyard. He was Major Tsuneishi of the Kempeitai. He seemed angry, his very personality seemed to be one of barely contained rage..."Orders!" he screamed..."You will obey orders or your lives will be forfeited!" We stood transfixed, it was a performance designed to intimidate and it was extremely effective. The interpreter translated the outburst, himself shuddering in the place of trying to duplicate the major's tone. The major narrowed his gaze and looked up and down the row at the wall. He angrily grunted, "Is there anyone who refuses to obey orders?" To most there it seemed like being captured all over again, with the threat of immediate execution a hanging in the air.

Captain Kalbfleisch, obviously an extremely brave man, stepped forward out of line. Guards quickly grabbed him and dragged him away. His small pile of personal belongings remained there on the ground where he had stood. The rest of us were told we would never see him again, and it was intimated that he had been executed. Years later those remaining would discover that Captain Kalbfleisch had survived the war, but for the time being, the charade had its desired effect, and from this point on, nothing would be quite as it seemed. The Japanese were attempting to manipulate us to the very core of our beings, and it would not be too long before we would begin to produce charades of our own. At this point, however, one thing had been established: no one remaining would openly disobey orders. We had no idea what those orders might be, but we were sure that they would be dreadful.

This was the middle of November 1943, and for the next two months, what we confronted was not so much dreadful as it was perplexing. It was not torture, or beatings, or slave labor, instead it was books and lectures. Nothing was said about our purpose for being there. We were brought books on Japanese geography, language, social customs, history and many tracts and pamphlets about the "Greater East Asia Co-Prosperity Sphere", the grandiose title for what would lay beyond Japan's successful conclusion of the war "...Asia for Asians..." ruled, of course, by Japanese. We were ordered, "Read!" So we picked up the books and made a show of reading. Everyday Japanese civilians would come in and make long and ludicrous lectures about the same topics. It was a crude and farcical effort at "brainwashing". It wasn't being successful in the least. We looked upon our lecturers as buffoons, and our guards as slow-witted psychopaths ...dangerous, but not at all effective at what they were trying to do.

The lecturers smiled a lot and attempted to be ingratiating, to what end it was not clear, and one day they brought in paper and typewriters and gave a simple order, "Write!" What it was they wanted written they did not say, but we had learned to make a show of doing whatever it was we were ordered to do, and exercising whatever original tangent we could misconstrue from the order. We wrote, all right: we wrote letters home, we wrote childhood memories, fantasies, menus, anything but the polemics we had been force fed. Our Japanese lecturers became furious at our feigned ignorance of what was expected of us. It was not entirely feigned; we didn't really get it. Up until this time, no one had mentioned, "radio script". Radio broadcasts were the farthest thing from anybody's mind.

We hadn't all arrived at the same time, but finally the population of Bunkwa Camp stabilized at around thirty. Each group had a similar performance by Major Tsuneishi upon their arrival. There was one Japanese/Caucasian boy from Texas, named Fujita who was much more a Texan than he could ever be Japanese, not knowing anything about the language and culture. He was a very fine artist. There was an American Lieutenant named George "Bucky" Henshaw from Hawaii; an enlisted man from New York named Joe Asterita; there was Larry Quille a civilian who was captured on Guam or Wake; a man named Shattles, a civilian, a graduate of Tulane University; a Dutchman named Schenk who became the group's cook; an American Master Sergeant Newton H. Light; a Navy man named Smitty (Smith); an Australian named Parkyns; "Leftenant" McNaughton of the Argyle and Sutherland Highlanders who had been a professional stage actor in England; a Scotch boy, Donald Bruce from Glasgow; and an American civilian named Mark Streeter who espoused some very strange anti-American views.

We prisoners had gotten to know each other, and the Japanese attempts at indoctrination were having no effect whatever. The elements of the Japanese efforts that were effective, of course, were the old standbys; threats of execution, beatings and starvation. We would follow orders in the most literal sense but with the minimum of cooperation. The Japanese responded by cutting our miniscule rations by twenty or thirty per cent. They increased the measure of brutality and held back food, both by measured degrees. And they increased the number of lectures.

One day the situation gained a new element. A taxicab pulled up in front of Bunkwa Camp and two Caucasians got out and entered the compound. They were well dressed and well fed and clean-shaven, but they were not at all at ease. They had the worried look of men under extreme pressure. I recognized one immediately, it was Captain Wallace Ince, whom I had last seen in Bilibid Prison in Manila. The other, I would learn, was Major Charles H. Cousens, from Australia.

The POW's were lined up on the second floor of the barracks building and we were called to attention as Cousens and Ince were brought in and introduced. Major Tsuneishi grunted to his interpreter who relayed in English; "These are your commanding officers. You will follow their direction. You will obey their orders." Cousens and Ince did not seem at all comfortable in their roles. It was apparent that they were acting under some heavy intimidation themselves. They gave us no orders. For several weeks they merely attended the lectures with the rest of us for two or three hours a day, then the Japanese would take them out.

Most of the POW's at Bunkwa were naturally suspicious of Cousens and Ince, arriving, as they did in taxicabs, dressed in civilian clothes and moving about without guards. Most of the prisoners would have little to do with them at first. Captain Ince and I, of course, recognized each other, and from our conversations, I became vaguely aware of what was going on. Ince had glowing things to say about Major Cousens, that he was a fine man and could be trusted. He said that he and Cousens had been broadcasting over Radio Tokyo for many months, though he didn't say what they had been broadcasting. Slowly it began to fit. The Japanese had been trying to get us to write material that could be used on their radio program. It was still not understood that the POW's ourselves were going to be used on the air. That was something that had no precedent. Propaganda radio broadcasts were something new to this "modern" war.

By the end of December 1943, Ince and Cousens had been instructed by the Japanese to begin making use of some of the POW's from Bunkwa Camp as broadcasting voices. We had never heard of such a thing. Several groups of POW's were taken down to the nearby studios of Radio Tokyo and returned in the afternoon. One day it was my turn. Captain Ince handed me the script I was to read. The script started: "This is the voice of Greater East Asia....Strong, courageous, perfectly united, ever victorious ...." It went on and on in this very heavy handed tone, extolling the virtues and sacrifices of the Japanese people in their historic war effort to unite Asia and throw off the yoke of Colonialism. This was totally unexpected situation to confront. Nothing in my memory had value as guidance. Nothing like this had been covered in my indoctrination or oath upon entering the military. Nothing in the fine military education I had received on Taiwan related remotely to this. The script filled me with revulsion and dread. "Captain Ince, I can't read this ...I'm not going to say this over the air." Captain Ince replied, "You are, or I'll have to let you face the Kempeitai...You must obey this order."

The Japanese controlled the basic facts of existence. A bullet waited for the disobedient, starvation for the resistant, beatings and malnutrition waited for all, in any event. My own superior officers, Ince and Cousens, whom I had sworn an oath to obey, even though it meant my death, did not order me to die, but ordered me to speak words into a microphone. Could I disobey? After two years of prison camp, survivors knew one thing; it was pointless and lethal to overtly disobey. Your resistance has to be sub rosa, beneath the surface visible to our captors, taking every advantage of the language barrier. I was driven down to the studios with a small group of prisoners. There were eight of us, I think.

Captain Ince knew every one of the studio technicians and seemed to be on very friendly terms with them. Ince controlled the program, cued the various parts when to come in, and had his hand on the controls. These shows were live on the air, not pre-recorded. They were powerful shortwave transmissions, beamed at the American public and allied forces in the field and POW camps. When it came time for me to read my portion, like most of the others, I did my best to screw it up: I gave words the wrong inflections, phrased sentences in an awkward manner, making it clear to any English speaking listener that I was not cooperating, and still maintained an appearance of acquiescence to the Japanese monitors following the script, syllable by syllable. Kempetai guards glared at us, reminding us that a price would be paid for any deviation. This was the saber's edge that the POW's of Bunkwa Camp danced on the entire 18 months on the air at Radio Tokyo.

Before the influx of POW talent of which I was a part, in March 1943, Cousens, Ince and Reyes had begun broadcasting the program "Zero Hour". At first, the Japanese had provided all the scripts. The scripts always needed heavy editing just to correct them in matters of syntax and vocabulary. Finally they had convinced the Japanese to let them write their own scripts.

Making the best of the situation meant making an outward show of cooperation in an effort to gain the maximum control over our own broadcasts and to subvert the intent of the program; to make it a morale booster to the Allied troops. We would keep the propaganda sections at their laughable pompous level and expand portions that contained genuine entertainment, music and news. They also included messages from POW's to their folks back home to say, at least, that they were alive. Where the news was of an adverse military or polemic nature the announcers would fall back on our basic subversion; the use of stilted phrases, mispronunciation and comic delivery.

It was at the studios of Radio Tokyo that Iva Toguri's path crossed with mine. She had been delighted to find some Allied military personnel in the building where she worked as a typist, and she would use whatever excuse she could think of to come into contact with us. She hungered for someone to share her pro-American sentiments with. All the other Japanese/American employees working at the radio station had renounced their American citizenship. She alone refused to do so, despite constant pressure from the domestic security police. It was she alone that openly wanted the Americans to win the war, and was thereby ostracized from genuine social contact with her co-workers. Cousens and Ince were very important to her.

In November 1943, Major Tsuneishi decided to expand Zero Hour, and Major Cousens, fearing that new announcers, especially female voices which couldn't come from our newly created POW pool, might prove to be the undoing of his tenuous grip on the content of the program, decided to recruit the obviously pro-American Iva for the expansion. She was reluctant at first, but Major Cousens was very persuasive. He told her that she would be actually helping the Allied war effort; that she should put herself under his command as if she were a soldier. Couched in these terms, she found the offer irresistible.

The scripts Cousens had written referred to her part as "Ann.", the abbreviation of "Announcer". She was worked into the program as Ann, and later Orphan Ann. She was a cheerful and joking disc jockey only reading the scripts prepared for her by Major Cousens; she never ad-libbed or read her own material. She did what she was told.

The Japanese were not entirely fooled by our first crude attempts to sabotage the broadcasts. Beatings were increased in number and severity and food withheld whenever our subversion became too obvious. Most of all, we objected to the strident pro-Japanese pronouncements required of us in "Zero Hour".

To get better control of the broadcasts, and get us off that particular hook, Cousens encouraged us to appear more cooperative with the Japanese by agreeing to write our own material. We were then allowed to create a program separate from the "Zero Hour" program, which could be adequately staffed by Cousens, Ince, Reyes and Iva Toguri. The program was called "War On War". Lt. Henshaw came up with the idea of a series that could be used in a number of ways to subvert the Japanese intentions. It was called "The Boys in Barracks Three", a prison camp drama serial. In it we all took parts as POW's (I called myself Leo) and described as best we could what conditions in the camps actually were. While appearing to the Japanese that we were saying that things were just fine, we put in words with double meanings, idiomatic phrases which would not be familiar to the Japanese and subtle intonations of sarcasm that would not show up in the scripts which were proofread by the Japanese before air time. In a few weeks we were confident enough to begin to insert information that could have military significance, the location of prison camps and especially weather reports over Tokyo.

We began to see ourselves as forward observers, intelligence operatives broadcasting from the heart of the enemy camp. We were certain that all the broadcasts from Radio Tokyo were being monitored on a 24 hour a day basis and analyzed by Allied intelligence. The government has never revealed if our efforts to communicate were understood or used, but to the POW's of Bunkwa Camp, it was an extremely important key to our morale. The belief that we were still a part of the Allied war effort, that what we were enduring, and the risks we were taking to get messages into the broadcasts had some meaning is the kind of psychological nutrient that allows the physical body to survive far beyond its normal limits.

U.S. bombing raids that seemed to appear on days when we had forecast clear skies over Tokyo reinforced the belief that we were being heard. When the B-29's appeared overhead, they were bigger than any planes we had ever seen. They seemed to me as big as apartment houses, literally hundreds of them. The Japanese ran for their bomb shelters, but we POW's went out into the courtyard cheering and waving, even when the impact of the bombs came within a few blocks. The nearby train station was totally obliterated, but the Radio station and Bunkwa Camp were never hit ...further indications to us that our messages were getting through and that Allied Forces knew our location.

Not long after the "War On War" program had begun, two new POW's were brought in who were fliers that had been shot down in the South Pacific. One was Lieutenant Jack King Wizener and Major Willeston Madison Cox. Once he had been told what was going on, Major Cox had an ominous comment to make: "When this is all over, you guys are going to get medals or get hanged." After choosing between starvation, beatings and possible execution for refusing and on the other hand malnutrition, fewer beatings and speaking scripted lines into a microphone under orders from a superior officer; Major Cox made the obvious choice. Months later, after he had taken his place with the rest of us, and air raids in Tokyo had become routine, he commented, "The best thing that could happen is that a bomb come down right here and save us the trouble of trying to explain all this."

"War On War" was expanded again and again as more POW's were brought to Bunwka Camp. In all there were over forty that were used in the POW broadcasts. One portion of the program was called "Your Missing Men". It had been part of "Zero Hour" but later became its own feature in expanded form broadcast by Bunkwa inmates. It consisted of messages from POW's from all over Japan. Of the thousands of messages brought to Bunkwa Camp only a small percentage could be used on the air. Those that were chosen for broadcast were those that indicated as much as possible, the location and size of the prison camps, and messages whose contents had double meanings.

The Japanese brought in a number of scripts of stage plays published by the Banner Play Bureau of New York, some of which had an anti-war theme. We were instructed to perform them as radio plays. In early March 1944, the first was broadcast..."Johnny Comes Home", an adaptation of Dalton Trumbo's "Johnny Got His Gun". Six or eight POW's participated in that broadcast. Thereafter, we performed "Journey's End", "Bury The Dead", "The Postman Calls", "She Met Napoleon", "Vision of an Invasion" and Steinbeck's "Of Mice and Men", in which I spoke the lines of the half-wit Lenny. Later in 1944, the POW program was renamed "Humanity Calls". In December of that year, we performed "A Christmas Carol". I played the characters of both Scrooge and Tiny Tim.

Several segments of the show were political commentaries and news, but I never participated in these portions, it just wasn't my forte. The news and commentary were laden with the double meanings that the POW's used in an attempt to communicate. The material that I myself wrote and broadcast was of a more poetic and mystical nature. So complex and obscure were my efforts to pass intelligence that they likely served more as decoys; forcing the Japanese censors to spend extra time microscopically examining my intricate scripts for what they might be saying. "The Moon and I" was one of my solo performances. When some day this all comes out, and recordings or at least transcripts of these broadcasts come to the surface, that's my voice; "The Moon and I", "Tiny Tim", "Scrooge" and "Lenny". I can't believe that Allied Intelligence was not listening to all these broadcasts and applying analysis to it. Records of those efforts must have been kept somewhere, if not recordings.

I can't say for certain that the Allies knew what we were trying to do, but our captors did, and for that we repeatedly paid a real price. The Japanese were aware of the POW efforts to use the broadcasts, but they could not identify them all. When they had a hunch we were up to something, we were harassed. When an especially suspicious effort was made, severe punishment was dealt out. The routinely brutal Kempeitai guards from Bunkwa accompanied us to the studio and stood by as Ince put us through our paces.

Cousens was the acknowledged commanding officer and helped the POW's with our scripts. He knew the technical aspects of voice and radio drama; and was especially valuable to us in maintaining our morale and our sense of being intelligence operatives. He also did what he could to take care of our physical health. At first, the Kempeitai would daily order the POW's into the courtyard for calisthenics and have us run laps, slapping or beating us for sluggishness or lagging behind. In our emaciated condition many fell or passed out from the strenuous exercises ...indeed there were many times when POW's fainted from hunger in the broadcast studios. Finally Major Cousens was able to take over the exercise period and give us a workout we could handle. Mainly, he gave us deep breathing and stretching exercises that would help maintain our vitality and not rob us of our strength.

In nearly 20 months of my confinement at Bunkwa Camp, I was just another one of the POW's. I had no special status by virtue of my linguistic capabilities. I made no effort to make my Buddhist priesthood known. I had used what I knew to play a Buddhist priest in a dangerous bluff on Corregidor. I knew just enough to play the part, but I was only a novice priest. I had taken a vow and embarked on the journey to become one, but I had just begun. There was however, an old Japanese couple affectionately referred to by the POW's as "Papa-san and Mama-san", who lived in the basement of the main building at Bunkwa. They had been janitors there when Bunkwa Camp was still a civilian "culture school". They felt sorry for us and did everything they could to help. I was close to them and I would often go down to their quarters to pray before their small shrine.

*   *   *   *   *

Iva Toguri had found comfort and purpose in working with Major Cousens and felt as though she were a soldier, or an intelligence agent. When the Bunkwa inmates were first brought in, she was horrified by our emaciated and ragged condition. Cousens, Ince and Reyes had been well enough fed, dressed in civilian clothes and quartered in private hotel rooms, coming and going without guards. The three were prisoners of war, but not abused to the extent that the rest of us at Bunkwa had been. Iva's portion of the "Zero Hour" program did not overlap the time when we POW's were in the studios for "Humanity Calls", but whenever possible, she would stall her departure, finding some excuse to come into contact with us. At great risk to herself, and material sacrifice, she smuggled us extra food or medicine that she had purchased on the black market, or saved from her own minimal ration. On at least one occasion she brought a blanket for a prisoner who had gotten very sick at the coldest part of the year. She always had a word of encouragement for us, and news of Allied war successes. There was an insolvable tangle of suspicions about one another at Bunkwa Camp, but none of us would have considered Iva anything but a heroic, patriotic American. Several of us likely owed our lives to her actions.

No one at Radio Tokyo ever used the name "Tokyo Rose". That was a GI legend. In fact, the use of Tokyo Rose, and sometimes Tokyo Rosa, goes back to at least 1937. It was a generic term for a female English speaking Japanese broadcast voice, as could be heard all over the Western Pacific. After the war began, Japanese began to use the radio facilities in their captured territories to broadcast sultry, alluring voices to suggest to the sailors, soldiers and airmen in the South Pacific that their wives and sweethearts were at home in bed with draft-dodgers. At least ten women were known to have used that style radio persona. Iva made no such broadcasts and no one has ever been able to produce recordings or even transcripts of her doing anything of the kind. Her voice is anything but sexy and alluring. Even the recordings of her disc jockey broadcasts used at the trial were of her unmistakable voice: a rough, almost masculine chattering voice ...a comic voice. Nonetheless, Iva was going to be accused of being the legendary non-existent seductress Tokyo Rose herself.

Stranger than anything that came before, in the early spring of 1945, everything began to change at Bunkwa. In the unfolding drama we glimpsed were decisions that would soon turn 200,000 people to ashes. I don't claim to know the details of these tragedies. Though we were uniquely close to the center of events, about 10 blocks from the Imperial Palace I can only testify to little known clues of the larger plot, and provide further mysteries.

Chapter Ten

Peace Crimes

Without announcement, a most unexpected change in the atmosphere of our circumstances at Bunkwa Camp began to reveal itself. The two Japanese civilians who had been in charge of the overall propaganda effort at Radio Tokyo were Ikeda and Domoto. Count Ikeda was the vicious and vitriolic one. He had been in a position of preeminence for the first year at Bunkwa. Domoto had always been smooth and conciliatory and now seemed to increasingly supersede Ikeda in authority. It was a welcome change but soon even more confounding.

Domoto had begun cautioning the POW's about the questionable parts of our scripts, rather than rebuking us and having us punished. He began to portray himself as part of a peace faction within the Japanese government that wanted to bring the war to a negotiated conclusion. He indicated that he was on very delicate ground with the military. The military had led Japan to wars of conquest and had vowed to fight to the very last drop of Japanese blood and never surrender. Domoto's actions would have been considered treasonous. He was in charge of our broadcast activities at Radio Tokyo; but we were always accompanied by our guards from the military police, the Kempetai, at the studios, and back at Bunkwa Camp.

Over a period of a few months, Domoto tried to convince us that he was responsible for the softening of our treatment by the Kempeitai. He would confide in us the growing sentiment of the government and let us know when our scripts were alarming the military censors. He let us know that he was aware of our efforts to broadcast double meanings and military intelligence. He went so far as to make the startling suggestion that the POW scriptwriters try to indicate to Allied intelligence that Japan was ready to talk surrender. Of all the unexpected and baffling events that we residents of Bunkwa had encountered, this was the most bizarre.

From where we sat in the heart of Tokyo, it seemed conceivable. The American bombing raids appeared over the city daily for weeks on end, hundreds of those enormous B-29's each day. By the summer of 1945, they flew lower and lower, since no Japanese warplanes remained to challenge them. The city rumbled with the sounds of their engines and their firebombs fell all around. The population had been decimated again and again. On our daily rides through Tokyo on the way to the radio studios, we could see the growing devastation, huge swaths of the city burnt to nothing. School children had been evacuated from densely populated areas to the countryside to preserve a generation. The population that remained trudged along with green complexions, emaciated faces and hollow stares of desperation. Domoto's assessment probably was true. It was as obvious to me that the war was nearly finished, as it had been obvious to me that it was about to begin in 1941.

Now, our Allied POW officers were in a strange position: while it was certainly good news that the Japanese wished to surrender, it is not appropriate for a POW to aid the enemy in a peace offensive, anymore than it would be to aid it in war. Your country may not want its adversary to surrender at this moment. That's above the pay grade of anybody at Radio Tokyo. The dilemma was the topic of many arguments between Domoto and our POW officers.

Throughout the summer, Domoto continued his campaign of ingratiation and began to insinuate that the desire to surrender emanated from the Emperor himself. As incredible as it seemed to us, the captives, that the Emperor was asking for our help, the idea soon gained some concrete and welcome credence: Our Kempeitai guards were replaced by members of the Imperial guard, the Emperor's own palace police. At Bunkwa, we had always been told that we would be executed in the end, in any case of invasion; we were now told that our lives were under the protection of the throne.

This change in the guards came only a few days after August 6, 1945, my 28th birthday. On this day, I was tending a flowerbed near the guards' quarters. It was something I had begun doing months before, when I realized that I could overhear and interpret what was being said over the Japanese public radio broadcasts. On this day I heard the announcement that the Americans had detonated a weapon of unprecedented destructive force over the city of Hiroshima, and much of the city had disappeared in a fireball.

In the days following, the machinery of the Japanese Government deliberated the details of surrender within the Imperial Palace, and on the morning of the detonation of the second atomic bomb at Nagasaki the cable of surrender was sent to the Allies. Surrender was not made clear to the Japanese people until August 15, when in an unprecedented broadcast the Emperor's own voice was heard over the radio, exhorting them to "endure the unendurable".

It's not as though the Emperor's voice had the power to end the war. Bombs still rained on Tokyo; in the distance, U.S. Navy guns blasted unceasingly the approaches to Tokyo Bay. The message to the Allies had to be received, studied, discussed, accepted, terms of surrender decided, a formal communication of acceptance drafted, approved, delivered and a plan of occupation set into motion. The Japanese still had to communicate with all its far flung forces the order to surrender, disarm its military defenses in Japan, put down insurrections of individual units large and small, and prevent its kamikaze squadrons from carrying out their sacred oaths.

And what of the prisoners of war? It had long been the plan to execute us all if the Allies launched an invasion of Japan; but the possibility of surrender and acquiescence to invasion had not been widely discussed. Perhaps we should be executed to cover the details of the atrocities that had been committed against us, and to conceal the identities of the perpetrators. The message of the Emperor, "The Voice of the Crane", did not end the war. It brought on a scramble of reorganization and retrenchment, and among the Japanese civilians, a nightmare of chaos and fear, as they learned that they faced imminent occupation and domination by the American monsters they had been taught to dread.

The population was a desperate and sickly swarm of humanity. Their city lay in flames and ruins, not knowing where to run, where to hide, what to eat, what to do; stumbling through the ashes of Tokyo, weeping, wringing their hands in fear of what lay ahead, scratching for nonexistent scraps of food.

At Bunkwa Camp, the mood was not exactly one of elation, but more of a relief from a long vigil endured; the sentiment shared was "...well, now it's over, the Allies have won, and now it doesn't matter if we as individuals survive. We have lived to see the end, the outcome of all our Pacific-wide efforts." The oath that each one of us in our own way had made on the day of capture, that somehow he would continue to struggle, by whatever means, until once again our own forces were in control, and the world was again set upright. Our individual fates in the next few days seemed of little consequence now that we all, collectively, had won. There was little assurance that we would survive, even with victory at hand. Food was not in any greater supply; indeed, not even the guards and the civilian staff at the radio station knew where their next meal was coming from.

There were also powerful incentives for those Japanese who concocted the idea of Bunkwa Camp and "Zero Hour". Those who created the system of POW broadcasts had much to hide: The entire process of forcing prisoners of war to broadcast under threat of execution constituted a number of blatant war crimes. We at Bunkwa would not be surprised if at this moment executions would be carried out to conceal those crimes. No one knew what to expect, captive or captor. No one had expected the end to come so suddenly, most had expected a bloody and protracted invasion of Japan; and no one could have realistically expected to personally witness the end of the war.

A few months before, in June, Cousens had briefed

everyone at Bunkwa, telling us that he would take responsibility for everything to do with the broadcasts. But now, there was a move afoot to lay off some responsibility on me, of all people, a bit player in the Radio Tokyo world. I don't know when Captain Ince's dark feelings about me began. We had been acquaintances briefly in Manila before the war. He was present and broadcasting from Corregidor and no doubt had heard of the suspicions of me in regards to Captain Thomson's execution, and had perhaps believed them. Next we had met in Bilibid Prison, where he told me of going on a "secret mission to Tokyo", and encountering him again at Bunkwa Camp and the studios of Radio Tokyo where he was one of my commanding officers.

Now in the face liberation he was concerning himself with how the circumstances and events of Bunkwa Camp and Radio Tokyo would appear to the U.S. authorities. Captain Ince had called a huddle in the officer's quarters at Bunkwa. They were studying a copy of the U.S. Constitution that was among their books. They were particularly concerned with Article III, Section 3:

"Treason against the United States shall consist only in levying war against them, or in adhering to their enemies, giving them aid and comfort. No person shall be convicted of treason unless on the testimony of two witnesses to the same overt act, or on confession in open court."

Obviously, all at Bunkwa Camp had drawn to us the suspicion of treason, from anyone who had knowledge of the broadcasts. Ince got busy at the typewriter carefully and creatively drawing a caricature of a traitorous John Provoo. Ince knew very well that I had been suspect on Corregidor and that the Counter Intelligence people would certainly want to talk to me after the war. Why not expand the role of this traitor in the telling of the propaganda broadcast story?

Ince, having arrived and begun broadcasting over a year before myself and forty other POW's arrived at Bunkwa, would be under suspicion for his own actions. Ince had been the first American pressed into this new form of POW slave labor. He had been, like the rest of us, in mortal danger and undeniably under extreme duress, but how would he explain having been well fed, comfortably clothed in civilian suits, and quartered in a hotel room? What did such a gloved hand incarceration suggest?

Throughout our experience at Bunkwa we believed what Cousens and Ince were telling us, that we were part of an intelligence operation. We needed to believe that. If we didn't, many of us would have refused, even under threat of execution. The one who did refuse to participate, Captain Kalbfleisch, was taken away and not seen again until after the war. We were told he had been killed.

Ince had been broadcasting for nearly a year before my fellows and I began our stay at Bunkwa Camp. We shivered in our rags in unheated barracks, and dined on miniscule portions of gruel. How would Ince explain his coming and going by taxicab, writing the scripts and political commentaries for innumerable radio broadcasts along the lines of the enemies' purposes. Maybe I was being set up as a lightening rod. If he was convinced of the rumors from Corregidor, which some on the scene had even attempted to murder me for, or for whatever reason, he had come to regard me as expendable. He inclined his creative talents to characterize my radio work, among that of all these others, as the work of a lone collaborator.

Ince typed up his report. It was Ince's finger that controlled the switch at Radio Tokyo; it was Ince's finger that cued the various POW's when to step up to the microphone and when to begin speaking; now it was Ince's finger pointing at me in accusation. After nearly two years of faithfully following Ince's orders, the Captain informed me that I was under arrest. I was thunderstruck.

What did being under arrest mean? I felt no more confined than I had for the last three and a half years, and I didn't believe that Ince's version of events would even be taken seriously. Naively, like Iva Toguri, I believed that I would simply tell what had happened on Corregidor and Bunkwa and how we had all struggled and endured all manner of torment and suffering, and how we had never turned our backs on our government, and how we had attempted to subvert the Japanese intentions on the air and pass information to the Allies. This report was a key link in a chain I will drag the rest of my life. This report would weigh me down with presumed guilt long before my side of the story could be heard. This book will be the very first time the whole odyssey has been calmly, thoughtfully told. I ask only that it be read with curiosity.

A week after the Emperor's surrender message had been broadcast; the Bunkwa guards let it be known that everyone, including Cousens and Ince, were being moved to Omori Camp. It was not welcome news. Since we were at last housed there, Omori had earned the name "Hell Camp", and the fliers who had been brought to Bunkwa after the rest had brought with them horrible stories about events there. We gathered up our meager belongings and the two complete scripts of all we had said over the air as POW broadcasters. We were loaded onto trucks and driven through the streets of Tokyo. The city was worse than ever before; few buildings remained standing, many were still in flames or smoldering and what people were in evidence scurried about, picked through the rubble, huddled in subway entrances and wandered in despair. The canals were choked with bodies of the dead. It would have been an easy bet that we would be exterminated when we reached Omori; before the liberation forces arrived and discovered the horrors and war crimes that had taken place there.

The trucks rumbled across the causeway to the island camp, Omori. They drove us past the camp headquarters where 20 months before, the Commander had absolved himself of our fate and consigned us to the Kempeitai. Trucks rolled to a stop within the compound ...there was no massacre in progress. Instead, the Japanese were hurriedly preparing for their own departure. Filling the trucks with the last contingent of guards, the camp was turned over to U.S. Navy Commander Mahrer, and the departing Japanese Commander addressed the assembled prisoners: "Remember the Japanese love flowers, children and POW's", and with that, he and the last of the Japanese left the island.

U.S. planes flew low over the compound and parachuted crates of food and supplies to the bedraggled throng. In their enthusiasm and the rush toward the descending crates several prisoners were crushed beneath them. Some of the final casualties of "Hell Camp", died on their day of salvation: some tried to swim out to the incoming barges and drown before they could be reached.

Captain Ince had lost no time in promoting his bizarre portrait of me. Immediately on arrival at Omori Camp, Ince had gone to Commander Mahrer and insisted that I be put under arrest. Commander Mahrer simply left the matter in Ince's hands. It didn't mean anything as far as custody or confinement it was just an idea in Ince's mind unofficially acknowledged by the Camp Commander, an annoyance to me on this otherwise joyful day of liberation, that I had no idea would be so short.

The liberating forces drew up to the island in landing barges and came ashore to the cheers of the surviving captives. The landing party was led by Commander Stassen. Of course, as soon as Ince got the opportunity he demanded that I be arrested. Commander Stassen refused, chuckling, "I don't know what any of you guys have been doing, arrest him yourself." When Ince did again recite his incantation, "You're under arrest". I snarled at him and stalked away. I never saw Ince again.

Among a thousand other liberated POW's, I was taken aboard the hospital ship Benevolence. Our rags were thrown overboard. We were disinfected with strong solutions and the weakest of us were taken to hospital beds. Those who could handle regular food were going to be sent back aboard liberty ships immediately; the rest would be nursed back to health before being repatriated. Someone asked me if I could make a chow line. "Sure", I said, and then collapsed.

I woke up in a hospital bed. A nurse came to my bedside and asked if I wanted to send a message home. I sent a short wire to my family to let them know that I was alive. The nurse returned with a set of earphones; I put them on and heard,"....drinking rum and Coca-Cola, working for the Yankee dollah." As she left, I noticed that I was in a locked hospital ward. It apparently was a psychiatric ward. There was someone locked in a small individual cell within the locked ward screaming over and over again, "Oh Lord my God, is there no help for the widow's son?" I would have gone crazy myself if I had to stay there much longer.

I was only in the hospital bed a few hours when armed MP's came and took me out, removed me from the ship and drove me to the outskirts of Yokohama and placed me alone in a cell in the old Yokohama Prison.

An officer came to my cell and said he was there to get a statement about everything that had happened. I thought that this was the opportunity to tell it all calmly and resolve all suspicions. I knew what light I had been seen in on Corregidor, but there had never been a forum to clear the air.

I began much the way this narrative begins; by describing my early childhood and my early interest in Buddhism and Japanese culture. I told him of my decision to join a Buddhist Sunday school and how I had always had Japanese friends. I spoke of the books I had read and how I had wanted to become part of a bridge of understanding between East and West...then I noticed that the officer had stopped writing. He narrowed his eyes and scowled at me... "You don't expect anybody to believe all this crap, do you?" I was thunderstruck once more. There was going to be no clearing of the air, not for a long time.

No statement at all emerged from this meeting, the officer

left with a few notes that he did not take seriously. This was the first of five or six dozen interrogations over the next seven years. It was typical of the interrogators I would confront. Ninety percent of my questioners would have their own answers to the questions before they even met me ...it would be an exercise in bending the interview into the same preconceived mold. An interviewer with an open mind was a rare exception.

When the officer left and I was alone again in my cell, I sank into a hopeless despair. I had been looking forward to this airing through all the years of the war. What a relief it would be to tell my story.

Just when life had seemed to exhaust all the possible visions of torment, the dark foreboding I had felt when Ince had first mentioned my arrest at Bunkwa was coming into focus. The years in prison camp had been an ordeal I had shared with my fellow POW's, the enemy was identifiable, the lines of conflict clear, and the Allied Armed Forces, of which we were a part, had been pressing relentlessly toward our rescue. Now the war had ended, the page had been turned, and the new chapter appeared, unbelievably, for me more agonizing than the last ...An ordeal to be faced alone, enemies within my own country's government, identities unknown; that enemy's motives and objectives, unknown; how to defend myself, unknown; who to trust, unknown; ...and who would come to my rescue: unknown.

Now I could see no resolution possible, not even the smallest fact about my past and my character was going to be believed. Perhaps I could salvage some victory from this tragedy by accepting responsibility, by taking the rap for my friends at Bunkwa. I was in this mood when General Eichelberger, Commanding General of the Eighth Army, came to my cell and looked in. "How are you son, are you going to be all right?" I blurted out, "General, I broke the chain of command." Eichelberger seemed to minimize my remark, "Don't worry, son. We're going to look into it." He seemed caring and sympathetic. It gave me a lift.

Yokohama Prison had been renamed XI Corps stockade by the occupation Army and was being used as a collection point for war criminals. I was in with some real ones. One was "The Butcher of Warsaw", Colonel Meisinger. There was another Nazi that had been the leader of the Hitler Youth Movement. I could see them through the barred window of my cell, walking around in the small courtyard where they were occasionally allowed to exercise.

On rare occasions, I was allowed in the courtyard and once there I encountered a sickly Japanese that I recognized. It was Field Marshall Terauchi, Commander of all of the Japanese forces in the South Pacific, to whom I had offered ice water three and a half years before on Corregidor, and who had spared me in my moment of daring, rebuking his forces for the treatment of the Allied captives. Terauchi said, "I know why I am here, but I cannot understand why you are here." Here was one who would have been willing to speak on my behalf, would it have done any good. He knew I was no traitor.

Then, just as suddenly as I had been put into Yokohama prison, I was taken out. I was put in a jeep, without guards and driven down to the Yokohama docks. I was told that I was going home and dropped off at the gangplank of a Navy Destroyer. It had just been a nightmare, a simple misunderstanding, simply corrected. I walked about the decks, a free man at last.

On my way into the mess hall, I ran into Mark Streeter, the loony advocate of technocracy. If anyone had been a crackpot propagandist at Bunkwa, it was this guy. He had no problem writing up and broadcasting really cockeyed anti-Roosevelt rants. He was the oddest duck there and really had no friends. We had enough shared experience to be glad to see each other. We went through the chow line, got our food and sat down at a table to talk.

We weren't there long when some sailors near us said, "Say, did you hear? There are some TRAITORS on board!" I swallowed hard. I had a strange feeling. The ship's Captain entered the mess hall with two armed sailors at his side, and approached the table where Mark and I were sitting. The Captain asked us to step outside. I replied that I could hear whatever it was right where I sat. The Captain became livid..."Arrest... Arrest ...Arrest these two!"

We were taken to the ship's brig, and placed in a very small cell. The nightmare was not over ...it was the freedom that was the fleeting illusory interlude ...I had awakened again into my nightmare. In the dim light of my cell in the hold of the destroyer at the Yokohama docks I wrote a letter of farewell to my family. At this point I felt that I would never see them again. I was deep in a hopeless despair. I had had cerebral malaria in the jungles of Bataan, been delirious from various tropical fevers, gone nearly mad from the suffocation and the vision of dead bodies floating in the sewage of the locked hold of the ship from Manila to Taiwan. I had been under the stress of imminent death for years on end and subjected to uncountable beatings and constant malnutrition. I had always been able to bounce back from my breakdowns and endure. But now I felt myself breaking, cracking and being twisted to an extent that I feared would finish me.

I was taken from the brig and driven to Tokyo, where Sugamo prison had been readied for the war criminals. I was placed in an individual cell on the third tier, with a steel door with a peephole in it. There were several Europeans, but Mark Streeter, Iva Toguri and myself were the only Americans held there. I was surprised and terribly dismayed to see Iva there, her of all people. She had been a heroine to us, and now she was being treated most callously, and being referred to as "Tokyo Rose".

On the heels of the occupying forces, came packs of reporters, sniffing through the rubble for the big stories. The Allied media didn't have a lot of specific names of the villains of the Pacific War and in occupied Tokyo there were two; the wartime Prime Minister, Tojo, and Tokyo Rose. The Allied Forces had Tojo, he was real and not accessible to reporters, and Tokyo Rose was a myth. The myth was determined to be a composite of voices from all over East Asia, a GI fiction. No one ever broadcast under that name under the 24 hour a day Allied monitoring through the entire war. The military issued a specific report to that effect. There never was a Tokyo Rose.

Among the journalists, were Harry Brundidge and Clark Lee, two who devised a strategy to stake a claim to the story of a Tokyo Rose, to find her and get the first interview. They offered the sum of $250 (a huge amount at the time) for an introduction, to whoever could arrange it. The trail led to Radio Tokyo and two male broadcasters, Oki and Mitsushio, who had worked on "Zero Hour". They were wary of the notoriety. Oki's wife was among the six girls at Radio Tokyo that had been used on air. They suggested that Iva, the one who had not renounced her U.S. citizenship and had been an outsider to the rest of the civilian employees at the station, might fill the journalists' requirements.

Iva was elated when the war was finally over and eager to make contact with the Americans who were everywhere in Tokyo. When asked to talk to these two, she quickly agreed to meet with them at their hotel. She told them quite bluntly that she was not Tokyo Rose but only the disc jockey sometimes referred to as Orphan Ann. She did want to tell her story and earn money to return to Los Angeles. Even though the truth didn't fit the lurid narrative already in the public mind, Brundidge, of Cosmopolitan Magazine, could see money in the exclusive rights to the story that could be portrayed as Tokyo Rose. He asked for her signature on a short contract, in exchange for which she was promised she would eventually receive $2000.

The other reporter present, Clark Lee of an International wire Service, however broke the story in the LA Examiner, with his own slant on the story: Shocking news that Tokyo Rose was a U.S. citizen, and that Cosmopolitan Magazine was rewarding her with a $2000 contract, which he dubbed "Traitor's Pay". The resulting public outcry put an end to Brundidge's dream, and brought pressure on the military to arrest her, which they did.

She was in a cell two tiers below me and directly across, so that I could see her when she stood at the front of her cell.

She was given no privacy at all, her cell had only bars on the front and her lights were kept on 24 hours per day. She was on display for the curiosity seekers, like a zoo animal. Many visitors came to her cell to stand and look, and to try to get her autograph. I was disgusted at the insensitivity of my countrymen. The spectacle being made of the courageous Iva gave me little hope that I would receive fair treatment.

I wrote letters home but my family did not receive them. The family wrote to me but I did not receive them either. I was not even given the letter that was to inform me that my mother had died. Finally my brother-in-law, a lieutenant in the occupation Army, managed to get in to see me for a short visit and tell me the sad news. My mother had survived the war and had seen all her sons return but one. I had been robbed of that victory over war, I had always dreamed of the day when I could see her again, after all that I had been through.

Of all things, Van Dienst was there: the white-maned Dutch Buddhist from Java, the one who had invited me to study in a Buddhist temple in Java years before the war. The Queen of Holland was petitioning to have him released, and in the meantime she had arranged for him to have a small organ in his cell, just a few doors down from mine. We would sing Buddhist hymns and chant Buddhist chants. It was wonderful to have him there, but fortunately, he was soon released.

Time after time agents of the Counter Intelligence Corps (CIC) came to my cell to interview me. I would greet them with hope or suspicion. They were mostly of the suspicious sort. When they showed a preconceived stance I gave them semi coherent ramblings and demands for counsel. When they showed any sign of listening, I gave them the truth. CIC agent

Milton Belinkie was one of those who listened.

I became friends with agent Belinkie. He believed me and sympathized with my plight. There were times when I was beginning to think that I would be able to get my story told. I even had reason to believe that I was being considered for being a CIC agent myself again. On several occasions, I was taken out of Sugamo and into Tokyo on various assignments. Once I was taken back to Bunkwa to describe what happened there. When we arrived there Mama-san rushed out to greet me and embrace me. She was glad to see that I had survived, was in good health and had even gained weight; she was happy to see an American face that she recognized among the thousands of occupation soldiers. The CIC agents even took me to their headquarters of military intelligence to translate Japanese language newspapers and to help in identifying Japanese guards that had been involved in various atrocities.

I had made friends with one of the G.I. guards at Sugamo and finally gained the support of Colonel Hardy, who was the commander of the prison. Colonel Hardy had become aware of the preconceived attitude of some of the interrogators and that their suspicions were not arising from the known facts ...something else was going on. He had a typewriter brought to my cell and told me to make my own statement, my own way, to take the time to tell it all and that it would get into the hands of the Commanding General.

On March 21st, I typed a 51 page single-spaced statement detailing the experiences of my war years. Within a few days, the Chief of the Legal Section of AFPAC recommended that no charges be preferred.

Early in April, a guard brought to my cell a brand new

Class A uniform. I changed and was ushered out of Sugamo Prison for the last time. I was driven to the Dai Ichi Building, headquarters for all the Allied occupation forces, and was taken to meet General Douglas MacArthur himself. He was an extremely busy man, but he took a minute to meet with me. The General said, "I wanted to tell you to your face. I wanted you to know that the Army didn't order your arrest and detention ...These charges were brought on instructions from high in the civilian government."

I was raised in grade to staff sergeant, given a statement that I had been cleared of all doubt or complicity and given passage on the next ship home. My Pacific war was over, April 4, 1946, eight months late.

Chapter Eleven

On The Double

It was hard to believe, but I was heading home; steaming toward Seattle on a liberty ship; in my new uniform, a staff sergeant in the U.S. Army. I had a statement signed by the Supreme Allied Commander, General MacArthur, that I had been cleared of all doubt and complicity, and that after an exhaustive investigation, no cause had been found warranting any charges whatsoever. My health was returning, my reputation restored and we faced a smooth spring voyage back to the U.S.

Several soldiers on board had served in the Philippine campaign and among them they had enough duplicate ribbons to provide me with the proper set of decorations, awarded by my new friends. We had great fun. I was free. Those few weeks aboard ship were some of the most untroubled times of my entire military career. All that suspicion and misunderstanding was disappearing behind me.

The ship docked in Seattle and the girl I had married four years before was waiting for me. I had only been in the United States for five weeks in 1941, returning from Minobu, then shipping out for Manila. Our relationship had been cerebral, long distance when I was a novice priest in Japan and of course conducted by mail. Our courtship and elopement upon returning was driven by the necessities of my abrupt departure.

She stood on the dock in her new leopard skin coat and embraced me when I got to the bottom of the gangplank. She had waited for me. A photographer snapped our picture for the newspaper. I was getting a soldier's welcome home from the war. She was ready to take up where we had left off, and was envisioning nursing me back to health in San Francisco. I was glad to be back and glad to see her, but my orders were to proceed to Fort Dix, New Jersey, and had only a few moments to share with her. We could get together on the East coast, and renew our romance. Up until then, our married life consisted of about two long weekends.

I was taken to a nearby military post along with the other soldiers that had been on board ship. We were organized into units and put aboard a troop train to cross the country. When we arrived at Fort Dix, I was sent to the finance office to straighten out my pay records for the POW years. The WAC Captain in the finance office insisted that I fill out claims for the jewelry, watch and personal effects I had been robbed of upon capture. I was allowed to draw $500 of what I had coming, while the Army sorted out the whole amount, and was given a weekend pass. My father and youngest brother, Robert, picked me up and we drove into New York for a weekend of celebration.

We checked into a first class hotel and spent the weekend dining, reminiscing and nightclubbing. At one nightclub in the Latin Quarter, the emcee began making a big deal about me being there in uniform, and the next thing I knew I was up before the microphone, saying how good it was to be back to the cheers of the crowd. It was my parade.

I returned to Fort Dix and was given more of my back pay, and assigned to 108 days of recuperative leave, which was standard for returned POW's. My wife joined me there and we drove down to visit my many relatives in the Southeast. I wanted very much to get in touch with my mother's family and her friends. It had been painful for me not to see her again and I wanted to sooth that hurt. I was beginning to heal emotionally. The end of my ordeal, once again, was an illusion.

There had been one irritating thing about my departure from Japan; I had to fill out a form requesting repatriation. I didn't understand that. It didn't seem like it would be necessary for a returning serviceman, and MacArthur's words, "...it wasn't the Army that did this..." hung in the back of my mind.

I was at my maternal grandmother's house in Virginia Beach, Virginia, when relatives from North Carolina called to say that the FBI had been there, looking for me. I drove down to North Carolina only to receive a call from Virginia Beach; the FBI had come there after I had left. I drove to the nearest military base and identified myself. I showed my identification, my orders, and my leave and told them what was happening. After a little checking, I was told, "You are to be held for trial."

It seemed the nightmare was on again. I was put in the stockade, and for two days I was held there, while my wife stayed in a motel just off the post. Then, suddenly, I was released. I was told that it had all been a mistake; that it was old orders that mistakenly hadn't been cancelled: that I was free to go and to forget it. By this time, it was not easy to forget.

I continued on my recuperative leave, but was approached by federal agents when I arrived at Fort Dix to pick up the remainder of my back pay. I insisted that before talking to them, we all go to the Judge Advocate's office where I could obtain some counsel. The agents balked at this and just said, "Well, we'll probably be back. We'll be seeing you later."

On August 17, 1946, I received an honorable discharge at Fort Dix, New Jersey, my wife and I left for San Francisco. We moved into a big, comfortable house in the City. My health was improving, slowly. My emotional state was deteriorating, however. I had a big worry. There was serious trouble coming from some faceless enemy in the government.

In Australia, Major Cousens was being put on trial for treason, and his explanations of the POW broadcasts were the same as they had always been to us. They were not being received at face value. At first he had denied that he had been housed in a hotel for a large portion of his time in Tokyo, or that he had exchanged gifts with one of the Japanese girls at Radio Tokyo. The prosecution was trying to paint him as a turncoat and if they succeeded, what could be made of the actions of the rest of us?

I became aware that a friend of mine, General Jones, whom I had known in prison camp on Taiwan, was the commander of the Army post at Camp Beale, California. I went for a visit. As soon as it was known that I was on the post I was sent right in to see the commander. General Jones rose from his desk to greet me and shake my hand, "You're just the man I wanted to see ...John, there's a conspiracy against you among the civilian authorities ...it's coming from cabinet level ...the best thing for you to do is to re-enlist, so that you will be assured of your military rights."

I needed little convincing, it was wonderful to think that I had some allies who knew what was happening and what to do about it. In the last four years, I had come to realize something; the POW years notwithstanding, I loved the Army. I wanted to experience it under better circumstances: when it was not at war, when there was food to eat, and when there was a chain of command that was in command. I wanted the discipline, and the camaraderie. On September 5, 1946 at Camp Beale, California, I re-enlisted for another three years.

My first assignment was to take a group of recruits by train across the country to Camp Lee, Virginia, and to be their sergeant through basic training. This was an ideal way for me to begin my regular Army career, since I had never had any basic training myself. I was able to stay on top of the situation and one step ahead of what the recruits were supposed to be learning. When this group of recruits finished, we all had the Army basics. They departed, and I was temporarily assigned to a housekeeping company.

At Major Cousens' trial Australia, Commander Bucky Henshaw had testified for the defense concerning events at Radio Tokyo and Bunkwa; and the proceedings were drawing to a conclusion, when suddenly, all the charges were dropped. The New South Wales Attorney General had withdrawn the charges on the recommendation of his superiors, the Solicitor-General and the Senior Crown Prosecutor, for undisclosed reasons. Trying to read between the lines, I surmised that perhaps the truth had come out but couldn't be publicly revealed. The following week, newspapers reported that the

Major had received an honorable discharge. Yes, I thought, everything had been straightened out.

Next I was assigned to Fort Sill, Oklahoma where I became the administrative head of the artillery school. I applied for Officer Candidate School but I was turned down ostensibly because of my age. One day my camp commander came to me and said, "Hey, what's this all about? There's a big pile of reports in your file and there's orders that you aren't to be raised in grade." The stress and the nightmare were still with me. The civilian government was interfering with my Army career. My enemies were phantoms. I wanted them to materialize so that they could be confronted. I needed an open hearing or a court martial so I could deal with it. I fell into an old habit of drinking heavily.

Newspaper reports from Australia early in 1947 were disappointing. Though charges against Cousens had been dropped and he received an honorable discharge, there remained a cloud on his reputation. He was being stripped of his former commission as Major, and denied the payments routinely made to returning POW's. .

I began to spend all of my off-duty time partying in nearby bars and enlisted men's clubs, and drinking to excess. In the daytime, I coached a boxing team, learned to fly a plane and took care of my Army duties; at night, I drank and partied. I began to realize that I had some problems that weren't going to be handled in this way. My legal problems, which wouldn't come out of hiding, were exacerbating some emotional problems that I couldn't hide from myself or cleanse myself of with booze. I felt that this high living at Fort Sill would eventually destroy me.

In the fall of 1947, I voluntarily entered Brooke Army Hospital at Fort Sam Houston, Texas, to break my cycle of debauchery. In the few weeks I was there, the most therapeutic thing that happened to me was the effort of a red-headed nurse, who brought me back to sanity in her own tender off-duty way. What she was able to do however was more than undone by a new round of interrogations by the CID (Criminal Investigation Division). It was the same old nightmare.

I had myself transferred to Fort Bragg, North Carolina so that I could get into the airborne. My old file of reports, charges and rumors followed me there, and the harassment, both official and unofficial, began to get uglier. The contents of my file were allowed to leak out, and I began to get open taunts and insults from soldiers I had never met; I was even beaten up by some who had no idea what the real story was or what a cruel tradition they were continuing.

My wife, alone most of this time back in San Francisco, had had enough. With little desire to follow me from camp to camp; to be a nomadic Army wife, she divorced me. Our marriage of 6 years had little for her to build her life around. I had returned from the Pacific covered with barnacles and pursued by monsters of the deep. It would have been too much for anyone.

I was thrown into the stockade along with another soldier on a charge of an alleged homosexual liaison, but the charges were dropped, when it could not be proved.

The pressure was making me increasingly agitated and emotionally unstable, and in the spring of 1948 I was sent to

Walter Reed Army Hospital. This time I was hospitalized for four months. Again, it might have been helpful had I not been regularly questioned by federal agents. It's difficult to shake your paranoia when you actually are being persecuted.

In August 1948, the Department of Justice made an official request to the Army that I be kept close to Washington, D.C. I was assigned to a headquarters company at Fort Meade, Maryland, with no regular duties. There was one good assignment during this period, which I relished. The Army put together a road show using Army personnel, and since I had some theatrical experience, I was made one of the directors. The show was called "On The Double", and featured a small band and a chorus of WAC dancers. We toured small out-of-the way Army posts in the South, traveling in two Greyhound buses. I even struck up a romance with one of the WAC dancers. It was a happy interlude in an otherwise dreadful Army career, but it was hardly an environment in which I could avoid alcohol. I drank constantly throughout the tour.

When the troupe returned to Fort Meade, I was again assigned to inconsequential housekeeping duties. In March, however, I was sent on an errand to the Federal Penitentiary at Leavenworth, Kansas, to return to Fort Meade with a prisoner. I was probably not the best person to be sent on this detail. Anyone who was a prisoner automatically had my sympathy. The prisoner was nearly finished with his sentence, and I liked him and trusted him. Before long the handcuffs were off and we were sharing a bottle of whiskey on the train. We proceeded to Fort Meade without incident, and the prisoner was delivered on time, though inebriated. Shortly thereafter, I joined him in the stockade, inebriated as well.

Nichijo

In addition to the obvious charges, I was inexplicably charged with sodomy. Nothing of the sort had happened on the train, and the Army ultimately would drop all the charges, but a second unsubstantiated charge of homosexuality had again been inserted into my service record. Charges from the train incident were used as a pretext to detain me most of the remainder of my Army "career".

On April 2, I was taken out of the stockade and hospitalized in the Psychiatric ward at Walter Reed, where I could be treated for alcoholism and the anguish it helped numb. The sympathetic and well-meaning doctors let me know privately that they were willing to open a way for me to take a side door out of my whole problem, to establish a defense of insanity. I was never one to slink away from my persecutors; what I craved was open confrontation.

The staff Judge Advocate at Fort Meade stated that it was not the policy of the Second Army to proceed against me because of the train incident since it was assumed that the actions were not criminal but the result of illness. The Army was more likely to have me discharged on a Section VIII hearing, a psychiatric discharge ...but the Justice Department didn't want me discharged in such a way, and not in Maryland.

Throughout April and May, I was interrogated at least five times by the FBI and often under the influence of some medication or another. I recalled being given a thick, dark pink elixir that seemed to have the effect of lowering my defenses, made me feel amicable toward my interrogators, helpful and cooperative. In this state I listened to recordings of broadcasts made at Radio Tokyo, and identified the voices speaking. The responses I made were typed up and I signed them on May 11.

On May 12, I was not given any medication and my memory of what had been happening in the preceding days gave me a lot to worry about. I made a formal request for military counsel because I was being investigated for and being threatened with the charge of treason. My request proceeded through channels. On May 18, I was told that my request was denied since I was not being considered for court martial. The military could not provide me counsel on matters concerning the Justice Department.

One might suppose that a man in my position would just completely crack up, and perhaps it was hoped I would. I didn't. I calmed myself. I didn't want to give them further excuse to hold me in the psychiatric ward with no charges. As always, I wanted them to get on with it, to raise the whole matter to public scrutiny, to confront the accusations in open court, where I had always been certain I could acquit myself if allowed to speak. It was only in silence and obscured from open inquiry that my persecutors had any power at all. I knew that there were literally hundreds of ex-POW's somewhere that could corroborate everything I said.

On June 2, I was released from Walter Reed and sent to the stockade at Fort Meade, ostensibly on charges stemming from the incident on the train. I was immediately granted counsel on these charges but since it had already been determined that these charges were not going to be pursued all the way to court martial, it was just a charade. Within days, my counsel was transferred to a distant post and I was promised that new counsel was being arranged. In fact, I did not get a new military counsel until August.

In the stockade, I was in contact with too many other

prisoners and guards to keep my situation quiet. Early in July, I was taken from the stockade under guard, and placed in a cell in the back of an abandoned firehouse. I was the only prisoner held there. I spent the next two months there, the remainder of my Army enlistment, held as completely incommunicado as could have been managed. Was it an unrelated coincidence that the trial of Iva Toguri was beginning San Francisco this very day? My commanding officer in Tokyo Major Cousens, and my accuser Captain Ince, had been called to testify in Iva's defense. Both told it exactly as it was, Iva was no traitor and a tirelessly selfless asset to the POW's at Bunkwa.

My guard detail at the firehouse had just one prisoner to watch, and little else to do. They did have instructions to perform a little drill, however, with a rather direct significance for me. It was target practice, actually, firing squad practice, conducted just outside the firehouse using a single man-size silhouette target.

I recall the unusual quality of some of the interviews the FBI conducted with me in the firehouse. The court record mentions twelve occasions during the month of August. I remember that several times the agents would arrive with an opened 7-Up bottle and would give it to me to drink. The walls of the firehouse, which had been rough, seemed to become smooth, and so did I. I felt smooth and yielding; I would calmly answer questions without embellishment, modification or explanation. I would sign whatever I was told to sign. The days following these interviews I would feel that the statements I had signed were misleading because of their brevity, and contained things I hadn't said.

As had happened so often in my long history of captivity,

I had made friends with one of my guards. I was able to get some messages out to my WAC girlfriend. The message was generally, "Help!" On one occasion, I asked her to contact one of the FBI agents that had been there the day before with the Seven-Up bottle: I wished to clarify some of the things I recalled saying. On another occasion, she managed to gain the ear of Senator Knowland, who was in a position to demand to know my whereabouts and status.

Efforts to resolve the situation were of no avail. Plans had apparently been made by the Justice Department. I was to be held without charges until the day my enlistment was up, September 2, 1949. Then I was to be subjected to a treason trial as a civilian. That last day in the Army there was a flurry of very odd procedures around mustering me out. It was a choreography of paperwork, legal gibberish and formalities, which I had no way of assessing at the time; not knowing how these obvious machinations served the purposes of my faceless nemesis.

September 2nd I was taken in handcuffs under military guard to Fort Jay, Governor's Island, New York, about 300 miles away. Among the many papers I was presented was my transfer from the Second Army, which included Ft. Meade, Maryland, into the First Army, Fort Jay. Moments later I was asked to sign a document accepting an undesirable discharge. I refused. Then I was given a direct order to sign; I did. The Army removed my handcuffs and removed the uniform off my back. FBI agents gave me a plaid suit to put on, then their own handcuffs, and led me to a waiting car.

Soon I was being driven though the streets of New York when I heard the FBI agents' instructions over their radio..."take him in through the front door. Don't let the reporters talk to him but give them plenty of time to get pictures..." Before we reached the courthouse, I was put in leg irons and chained around the waist and through the cuffs. As I was led up the front steps, my leg irons wouldn't allow me to make the step and I had to hop. I was led into a hearing room.

I was doing my best to make light of the situation and put the FBI agents at ease, but when the U.S. Commissioner entered the room and sat down things took a more serious tone. I still naively saw this as my opportunity to clear the air; finally something could be confronted, in public. I started to speak, but the Commissioner broke in immediately..."I advise you not to speak ...don't say a word." The Commissioner read the prepared arraignment. I was being charged with treason, and since the maximum penalty was death, I was to be held without bail. I stared intensely at the Commissioner, aghast, the words of the arraignment hanging ominously in the air. I never believed that the government would carry its misconceptions this far. Now I could see how deadly serious they were.

The Army had been a comfort to me, an extended family. But the Army had not been all-powerful; it had to maneuver around and finally acquiesce to civilian authority. After all, this is America.

Nichijo

Chapter Twelve

Wretched Refuse

427 West Street, New York City is an old three story brick Bastille near the docks. Supposedly, it houses society's worst for their crimes against the Federal Government. In my three and one half years awaiting my speedy trial, I met a few villains on the inside, but the real villains most often appeared to be those on the outside, preparing cases against them. I had long been predisposed to sympathize with the imprisoned.

I was taken to West Street immediately following my hearing before U.S. Commissioner MacDonald, and placed in an isolated cell. For the first few weeks, I didn't meet any of my fellow "detainees". I had been led into my cell; my chains and leg irons removed, and the cell door closed behind me. I sat down on my bunk, a piece of paper in each hand; one was an undesirable discharge from the Army, the other, an indictment for treason.

Freedom did not appear to be in my future. The only freedom available to me was that freedom I had glimpsed in the face of the Buddha in Golden Gate Park, had followed to Minobu and perfected during the long years of prison camp. I reflected that this freedom of the spirit was the only true freedom there is, and I, if anyone, was aware of how real this freedom could be.

Still, I determined to struggle against the legal bonds that held me, and reviewing the history of my treatment at the hands of my own countrymen, I could feel the as yet unconquered rage within me. I would catch myself, this rage was the threat to my inner freedom: it would not defeat my tormentors; it would more likely destroy me. It would take carefully calculated action to extricate myself from this trap, not emotion.

I could still rise to the blissful illuminated heights within. I could still plunge to the depths of despair over my outward circumstance.

For the first week, alone in my cell at West Street, I was allowed no phone calls, only a few telegrams to let my family know where I was. On September 9, I was taken out of the cell and taken again before a U.S. Commissioner. A Legal Aid attorney was there to advise. The prosecution team asked for a delay and my attorney did also, asking that I be allowed the use of a telephone to arrange the appropriate legal counsel. The delay was granted and the use of the phone approved.

I was returned to West Street. My cell was on the second floor, directly across from the guard station where, apparently, I could be watched until I was better understood. Perhaps I would try to commit suicide, or display violent tendencies that could endanger other inmates or whatever.

A man named Soares was the guard Captain. He was getting to know his new charge. It wouldn't be long before we were friends. It was always thus in my worst predicaments: an ally appears among my captors.

I was given the job of chipping the old paint off the bars of my cell in preparation for repainting. It was something I could do while in my initial close confinement to earn a little spending money for cigarettes. In a few weeks, I was placed in the cellblock where I would be in contact with other prisoners and the guards would treat me more routinely.

One of the most disturbing elements of my situation was appearing almost daily in the newspapers. The trial of Iva Toguri was in progress in San Francisco. Though Major Cousins and Captain Ince had testified in her behalf, it was not going well. On September 29, she was found guilty of one of the treason charges against her.

That day, I was appearing again before a U.S. Commissioner. This time I had a lawyer named Hornstein, who had volunteered to stand up for me until adequate counsel could be arranged. He was a Colonel in the Army Reserve and had formerly been a presiding judge of the General Court Martial in Europe. With him was my WAC girlfriend, Elizabeth McLaughlin. The government was asking for another delay so that they could bring the witnesses from Japan, that were being used in Iva's trial, to New York to testify before the grand jury indicting me. Delay granted.

A week later, Iva was sentenced to ten years in prison.

If they could do this to the loyal Iva Toguri, who had taken so many risks to help us: me and my fellow POW's at that diabolical Bunkwa Camp, what chance did I have? I held little hope that I would ever escape my situation alive. It was being a prisoner of war all over again. But, understanding that, I knew how to deal with it. I had spent three and half years as a prisoner of the Japanese brutal military machine, never believing that I would live to see the end of the war; and so, I had learned to function with goals that didn't assume that I would survive. There is a certain freedom in actually abandoning your own physical existence. I had done so over and over again since 1941 and now, I found myself in a dire predicament again. Each time, finding that I had survived, the cloak of mortality had descended over me again, renewing my attachment for living, and with it, the belief that I had something to lose. Now I was free again, free to act fearlessly, the freedom of the doomed.

This determined my whole approach to the matter. Above all, I had to continue to serve my fellow POW's. I would not defend myself by testifying against them, or mentioning the treasonous intentions of some of my accusers. I would not use in my defense any excuse of duress or insanity. To the best of my ability, I would not allow any of the other POW broadcasters to take responsibility for acts that would condemn them. I realized that Iva, cast as the legendary "Tokyo Rose" was the most exposed member of the Radio Tokyo crowd, and she had been the first to be prosecuted; and I was the second. If I was easily convicted, and named others in an effort to save myself, they would follow.

I vowed that, if nothing else, I would give the government such a long and expensive contest that even if convicted, the government would hesitate to proceed against the others. With that in mind, I could abandon my own fate, but not that of my friends.

In the middle of October, the government won convictions of eleven prominent American Communist Party Leaders under the Smith Act. The U.S. Attorney John F. X. McGohey and his assistant Irving Saypol, who had prosecuted them, had earned promotions. On November 1, Saypol was made the U.S. Attorney for the Southern District of New York, and his former boss McGohey, along with three others, Kaufman, Noonan and Sugarman, were made Federal Judges in the same district. Among them, presumably, was the judge from whom the Justice Department could "get cooperation", as alluded to by Justice Department attorney Noel E. Story, in his conversation with the Pentagon in August.

The Federal Grand Jury met in secret to put together the indictment against me, and when they had concluded their work, they insisted that the record show how much the jury had appreciated the manner in which Mr. Saypol and Mr. Story had made their presentation of the testimony.

The eleven convicted Communists were brought to West Street to await sentencing. They were out on bail within three weeks, but I got to know a few of them; especially Gus Hall, Ohio Party Chairman, Eugene Dennis, General Secretary of the Party, and Robert Thompson, New York State Chairman. I didn't care for their politics, but they were intelligent and good company. Much later I would see a man attempt to murder Robert Thompson with a lead pipe in the chow line at West Street.

It was a good season for Federal prosecutions and we were witnessing conviction after conviction as the celebrated accused paraded through West Street. We had a saying at West

Street..."Here we are, the refuse of the country, awaiting disposal".

Alger Hiss was there, in the middle of November, awaiting the beginning of his second trial.

On November 17, the newspapers reported that Herbert Burgman had been convicted of treason in Washington, D.C., for his wartime broadcasts from Nazi Germany. He was sentenced to twenty years.

On November 22, I was taken before Judge Gregory Noonan and the U.S. Attorney Saypol read the indictment against me. I was charged with twelve overt acts of treason: That I had voluntarily offered my services to the Japanese after the fall of Corregidor; that I had attempted to persuade a POW to give up secret codes and ciphers; that I had ordered a POW to give up his boots to a Japanese officer and had struck him and beaten him; that I had advised a POW to reveal the location of $7,500,000 in silver; that I had reported Captain Thomson to the Japanese, which resulted in his execution, that I had informed on fellow POW's on Taiwan; and that I had participated in at least six propaganda broadcasts from Radio Tokyo. I calmly denied the charges, and said that Saypol had presented an entirely distorted picture of events that had taken place 7000 miles away, seven years before. I was mystified how the government could possibly undertake to prove this version of events.

My attorney, Mr. Hornstein, entered a plea of not guilty, and argued for bail. Judge Noonan denied bail and ordered I to be sent to Bellevue Hospital for a complete physical and psychiatric examination, at the bequest of the prosecution.

For the next two weeks, I was in a locked ward at Bellevue. The surroundings were nicer in a way, and the food was better. I was examined by the famous psychiatrist, Max Wexler, a personable man who looked rather like Albert Einstein. After extensive interviews, Dr. Wexler said that I was as sane as anyone else that would be in the courtroom, and wrote in his report to the court that I was educated, cultured, well integrated but depressed, understandably, given my predicament. All he wanted to know was: "How did you ever get into this mess?" If there was an opportunity to take the easy way out via insanity, this was it. Instead, I presented my most stable and refined facade. I was returned to West Street in time for Christmas.

Isidore Hornstein had volunteered his services in my defense without fee, but even so, there were anticipated court costs of $10,000 to $15,000, which he had no way of covering. Also, he was beginning to realize that the scope of the case was beyond the capacity of his law firm to handle. He informed me that he would remain his counsel of record, and handle preliminary matters until adequate representation could be found.

Several lawyers had offered their services, but as I interviewed them I discovered that I wanted none of them to represent me. Most assumed that the indictment was correct, and wanted to create a defense based on duress and/or insanity. I would throw them out. It was depressing, but something more depressing was coming.

Within the deposition of one of the anticipated prosecution witnesses was the startling revelation that I had been a suspected traitor even before the war had begun. It was revealed that because of my unconcealed belief that Japan was being antagonized into confrontation by American economic sanctions, and my open adherence to Buddhism, that my loyalty was suspect. Military intelligence, of which I had been a part, had been gathering information on me in Manila, and during the last month before the fall of Corregidor, the MP's had orders to shoot me if I appeared to be signaling the Japanese. I had risked being killed by my own forces each time I left the tunnel to recite the Lotus Sutra from the hilltop during bombing raids: I had felt some covert hostility from the sentries at the time, but I had regarded it as the accustomed religious prejudice. I could see now, deeper roots of the rumors that seemed to spring up so quickly during the early days of Japanese occupation. The revelation was devastating news to me.

It was in this frame of mind that I appeared in court March 7, 1950. Mr. Hornstein was asking to be relieved from the case. Judge Medina was outlining a plan in which I would be assigned two attorneys by the court at the government's expense. I stood up and said despondently, "If I have anything to say about it, your honor, I would rather dispense with counsel and plead guilty." This caused quite an outburst in the courtroom. Mr. Hornstein was on his feet insisting that I had a good defense and was only acting in despair; that I had been changing my mind like this in recent weeks. Even U.S. Attorney Saypol objected to my making the plea while I had no counsel.

Judge Medina ruled that he could not accept my plea on an impulse. I replied, "It is not an impulse, I have been thinking about it for some time. I have been a long time getting justice; when my superiors in the Philippines lost confidence in me, I was dead."

A dapper Italian gentleman, Peter Sabbotino, stood up in the courtroom. "Just a moment your honor, I'll defend this man." One member of the prosecution team snapped, "Your honor, this attorney is just trying to jump on the bandwagon for publicity." Sabbotino turned to the young attorney, "I will have you know I was a quasi officer of the court and a former magistrate in this jurisdiction. I demand an apology." Judge Medina said firmly, "You certainly will apologize to the honorable Mr. Sabbotino."

As always in my darkest moments, an ally would appear from an unexpected quarter. Sabbotino's offer was accepted and I felt my hopes renewed.

During the next three weeks, I had a number of interviews with prospective attorneys to add to the defense team, but with much the same results as before. Finally I found two that I liked very much, George Plotkin and his wife Clara Storper. I was impressed by their realism and their belief in my version of the events listed in the indictment. Plotkin described the trial that we faced as a very heavy situation that was going to be very discouraging at times, but that they would succeed, "There is justice in this country, but you have to fight like hell to get it."

The Plotkins' support buoyed my spirits even higher and gave me the will to struggle, and the glimmer of a belief that I might overcome the entire set of accusations.

Another event raised I spirits even further. One day I heard a familiar voice chanting on the sidewalk outside West Street. It was the voice of Bishop Nippo, my beloved master who had accompanied me to Minobu in 1940.

"Namu Myoho-renge-kyo", he chanted, finding a tone that resonated against the grey brick walls. Inside, I began chanting, too.

Nippo had come all the way from Argentina, having heard of my plight through the international press. He had come as soon as he found out that I was in trouble. He had gone to the authorities at West Street and identified himself as my spiritual advisor, but had been told that they had spiritual advisors on the prison staff, a Protestant and a Catholic, and that was all that were allowed in the facility. In their minds, that seemed to cover all bases. Nippo returned to Argentina without seeing me, but just our voices resonating through the brick walls and iron bars had been an uplift.

I did get to know the Catholic priest that was allowed to meet with the prisoners. I told him everything, my whole life story, my entire religious history and war experiences. The priest became convinced that I was innocent of the charges against me and that I was suffering from some dangerously naive assumptions. "My son, you have made a terrible mistake: You have mistaken the government for Almighty God. They are poles apart." I had. I had always assumed that the government was a fatherly, omniscient entity, which would ultimately determine the truth and then do the right thing. I thought that upon a thorough hearing, the facts would come out, and I would be exonerated.

I gained other illuminating insights from the priest, but this was the most relevant to my present situation. We seldom talked about religion, per se, but at times we did; and during the course of our friendship, I received the blessing of the

Roman Catholic Church.

For the remainder of 1950, the defense team worked on preparing for trial. Over 700 potential witnesses were on their list, and they needed to be found, contacted, and depositions taken before the prosecution's team could get to them. In this effort I had the invaluable help of the American Bar Association, and various POW organizations. By the middle of August, they had completed most of those contacts and needed only to get affidavits from witnesses residing in foreign countries. There were sixty-two in Japan. The government expressed resistance to the idea citing the expense. Later a compromise would be reached where a much smaller number of witnesses would be contacted and only preliminary statements would be obtained, by long distance.

In January of 1951, the government requested a further postponement of proceedings, because their team was in Japan taking depositions from their witnesses.

I got to know many of the inmates at West Street; more communists, tax evaders, deportees, immigrants who had attempted to smuggle their family heirlooms past customs, junkies and drug dealers; the camaraderie of crabs caught in the same net.

I looked forward to the visits of the Plotkins' especially. Attorneys were among the few people from the outside that I was allowed contact with. When they could, they would bring me a pastrami sandwich and vanilla milkshake.

I painted two oil paintings as gifts for them: one of the Kuonji Temple at Minobu and the other a portrait of the founder, Nichiren. The Plotkins became aware of my blind side, as had the priest. I showed an unwillingness to believe that the government could act with malice, I clung to the idea that the government was trying to discover the truth. George Plotkin told me, "You've got to disabuse yourself of the idea that you're going to get a fair hearing; you are not." And I said, "You mean it's like war." Plotkin replied, "Now you've got it!"

I began to spend more time in the law library, studying the cases of treason and the various defenses available. I began to work up some of my own motions and to get more involved in the nuts and bolts of my legal proceedings. My rapport with Guard Captain Soares was invaluable for this effort. Soares allowed me into the library after hours where I could work on my case late into the night, with good light and a typewriter. The Captain also gave me a job in the basement laundry so that I would make extra money and have some freedom of movement within the building.

In the early part of 1951, U.S. Attorney Saypol was busy with another case and I soon met the defendants, Julius and Ethel Rosenberg. I was in touch with both of them. I would see Ethel as I went downstairs to the laundry, and through the wire divider of the rooftop exercise yard. I liked them both. At worst, they were misled, idealistically soft-brained, at best, they were what they had intended to be in their hearts: They hadn't passed along atomic secrets for money or personal gain; they had done it out of a desire to balance the world's power. They had thought it too dangerous for one superpower to hold so great an advantage. They had quixotically taken it upon themselves to correct it.

The presence of the Rosenbergs at West Street brought on an ominous and melancholy atmosphere. They, such gentle people, were being slowly, unceasingly prepared in the press and the courts, for the electric chair at Sing-Sing. In the evenings the whole building could hear Ethel singing Madame Butterfly from her cell. Their trial was held in the month of March 1951, and they were convicted on March 30. A week later they were sentenced to death by electrocution. A week after that, Ethel was moved to Sing-Sing; and Julius, "Rosie", followed her there in the middle of May. It would be two years before they would be actually executed.

My efforts in the law library had produced a writ of habeas corpus asserting that the government had no jurisdiction in the case since I had been illegally separated from the service, that I was still in fact in the Army and therefore subject to the Uniform Code of Military Justice. On March 16, the writ was dismissed and the trial date set for May 18, 1951. It was delayed again. My defense team was completely ready for trial by the summer of 1951. The fifteen-month delay before the beginning of my trial was the result of motions by the government.

In July, a prisoner was transferred from the Penitentiary at Leavenworth, Kansas for legal proceedings in New York. His name was James Martin Monti. If anyone in WWII had had a more bizarre set of experiences than me, it was Monti. He had been a U.S. Air Force officer in India, and one day he had an inspiration about how he might bring the war to an early conclusion. He hitched several rides aboard military planes until he reached Italy, where he stole a USAF fighter and flew it to Berlin, where he attempted to persuade the astonished Germans to surrender. The Germans chose to humor him and use him as a propaganda broadcaster. "Yes," they said, "we want peace. We want you to go on the radio and tell the Allies we want peace." Monti was eventually given a German uniform and regular duties broadcasting propaganda. Obviously, at the end of the war, he was in a lot of hot water with the American military. He had pleaded guilty to treason and had been sentenced to twenty-five years. His presence at West Street was part of an attempt to withdraw his guilty plea. I listened to his whole story. I felt very sorry for him, he had sincerely believed that he could get them to surrender.

Monti 's legal attempt had been unsuccessful and he had been returned to Leavenworth. I was sent to Bellevue for evaluation prior to trial, which at that point was scheduled for September 5, 1951. It was a routine observation period at the request of the prosecution, and it meant another delay in the start of the trial. For over a year more the prosecution would exhaust every imaginable excuse for delay.

Finally, ten years after the events on Corregidor, for which I faced the death penalty, the trial began. In that ten years, I had spent three and a half years in Japanese prison camps; had been held for eight months without charges or counsel in postwar Japan; had spent three years under a cloud in the Army, the last six months of which I was held without charges or counsel in military stockades; and a full three years at West Street without bail awaiting trial.

"Here we are, the refuse of the country, awaiting disposal."

Chapter Thirteen

End of the Tunnel

It was finally October 27, 1952, when my trial actually began: a little more than ten years after the fall of Corregidor. Judge Noonan ominously excused 40 potential jurors because they opposed capital punishment. Seven women and five men were ultimately chosen as the jury. I was satisfied with them. They seemed honest and intelligent people.

At the West Street law library, I had given myself a quick course in constitutional law. The U.S. Constitution requires that in order to find someone guilty of treason, two eyewitnesses to each overt act must testify in open court, or the defendant must make an open confession, in court. Statements made outside the courtroom may not be used. Rules of law also require that the prosecution prove that there was a willing intent to commit treason. Treason may not be constructed by the definition of an observer, treason must arise from within the motives of the traitor, and he must be shown to have been in his right mind, and not acting out of duress, in fear of his life or under threat of physical harm.

The prosecution's task then, is a clearly defined and definite procedure. Two witnesses must be found to testify to each overt act. The defense, however, has a much more difficult task: what omniscient witness could testify that any given act never occurred? Only the defendant, of course, knows the facts. The defense must rely on witnesses of the sort that, knowing the defendant and the circumstances, would know that the acts were unlikely to have occurred, or occurred in ways that were misrepresented by the prosecution. The defense may also attack the testimony of the prosecution witnesses on its accuracy as recalled; its vindictive bias against the defendant because of events not in themselves treason; or by inference that the testimony is perjured because of bribery, coercion or vendetta. The defense may also seek to excuse the defendant because he acted under duress, or that he did not know right from wrong at the time the acts were committed.

Anyone who has made even a cursory study of Japanese treatment of their POW's in WW II would have to agree that there couldn't have been any POW that was not under duress for the entire term of his captivity. The Japanese forces were the most brutal in history.

In 1937, at the outset of their conquest of China, the Japanese high command made a monstrously callous effort to establish a reputation of unearthly terror which in itself would be counted among their weapons of war, a weapon which could be referred to in the polite chambers of American jurisprudence as "duress".

As they closed in on the old Chinese capital of Nanking, contending factions within the Japanese military were promoting opposing policies of occupation to their superiors. One faction maintained that the victors should demonstrate benevolent administration of the conquered city, thereby encouraging the easy surrender of the conquests that lay ahead.

The other faction held that the occupation should be a demonstration of such utter horror and butchery to punish the considerable resistance that had been offered, that potential defenders of future conquests would dare not oppose them at all. The latter argument was adopted as policy.

From the middle of December 1937 to the middle of January, 80,000 Japanese troops were turned loose in Nanking to systematically do their worst. By the end of that horrible month, the massacre of the surrendered and unarmed captives amounted to well over 100,000. They, and an additional 50,000 hapless civilians were murdered by every imaginable means; shot, beheaded, burned, buried alive; drowned, smashed and dismembered. Thousands were tied to stakes and used for bayonet practice, so that young Japanese soldiers might overcome their squeamishness about bayonetting living people. Over 20,000 Chinese women were mercilessly gang-raped and often murdered when they became too pitiful to be of further service. This hideous episode well established the desired reputation.

During the siege of Singapore in 1942, Japanese troops penetrated British lines and overran a hospital. They massacred nearly everyone including the patients, which they bayonetted in their hospital beds.

After the fall of Bataan, 70,000 American and Filipino captives were marched sixty-five miles to the north without food or water. Emaciated from months of miniscule ration and sick from numerous tropical diseases, they were bayoneted or beheaded if they fell behind or offered any resistance to orders. 10,000 had been killed in this way while the battle for Corregidor reached its conclusion.

The story of Allied POW's in Japanese hands is one of summary executions, arbitrary beatings, death by starvation, diseased prisoners being worked to death under the gun, and even incidents of cannibalism. Any POW accused of treasonable acts could have easily established a defense of extreme duress.

To me, the matter of a defense based on duress was out of the question. None of the allegedly treasonable acts on Corregidor had occurred, and the radio broadcasts were made under the orders of superior officers. Whatever the penalty threatened, I could not bring myself to consider that sort of defense. The attorneys who showed enthusiasm for the prospects of acquittal on these grounds were shown the door.

Likewise, I regarded the insanity defense out of the question. When I was six years old, I had fallen from a second story balcony onto a concrete courtyard and had fractured my skull. I lay in a hospital bed for a week, unconscious. It was doubtful that I would recover at all, and if I did, I would likely have suffered permanent damage.

All my life, I seem to have exhibited an emotional volatility and an exaggerated sense of seriousness about my inner conflicts. In 1939 I had visited an "alienist" for advice about my conflicts.

On Bataan, I had contracted cerebral malaria and it been testified to that I suffered breakdowns on Corregidor and at Bilibid Prison. I had been in and out of psychiatric wards throughout my postwar Army enlistment. Army doctors had repeatedly offered me the "side door" out of my troubles. In short, I could have easily documented a defense of insanity, but I would not. I had no need of such a defense; I had acted courageously at every turn on Corregidor, and from Radio Tokyo, I had broadcast under orders from superiors.

Even the prosecutors had provided repeated opportunities for me to avoid trial by reason of insanity, but when I was sent to Bellevue and to Staten Island, I was careful to do everything I could do to demonstrate that I was sane, sane enough to stand trial, and sane enough to face the indictments and denounce them as false.

Of the twelve original acts in the indictment, five were thrown out by Judge Noonan before the case went to the jury. Of the seven that remained, the jury could only agree on four. They found me guilty of offering my services to the Japanese, contributing to the death of Captain Thomson and participating in two radio broadcasts.

Many of the witnesses against me probably believed that I had been working for the Japanese. Some had been so convinced at the time that they had privately asked me if I would help them offer their services to the Japanese. They had no doubt been embittered by my tacit refusal to do so. They all had three and a half years of the deprivation of prison camp to nurture the idea that I had made a deal with the enemy for myself, and not for them. One had attempted to murder me in my hospital bed by injection of a lethal overdose.

Many testified to their rumor-based bias and hatred for me prior to the time when they had allegedly witnessed any overt act.

Two testified that they had believed me to be disloyal

even before the fall of Corregidor.

Two of the prosecution's witnesses became witnesses for the defense.

Two pairs of witnesses in the Captain Thomson incident contradicted each other about details that should have been plain.

Two witnesses told of me nearly being beheaded by Japanese officers in two separate incidents; odd, that the Japanese would be so willing to kill such an allegedly valuable collaborator.

To be fair, it must be said that whatever creative testimony was presented by the prosecution witnesses, might have been the work of individuals who believed me guilty, and determined that I would escape punishment if they didn't create eyewitness accounts of events they believed to have happened.

One was an American officer in military intelligence on active duty at the time of the trial.

Several of the witnesses had been brought from Japan. To them, an all expense paid trip to New York must have been a very attractive prospect.

One of these witnesses was taking a vacation from a sentence of thirty years at hard labor for his war crimes. Incredibly, he was the Japanese sergeant who actually killed Captain Thomson.

One, Ruth Hayakawa, had been an English-speaking broadcaster at Radio Tokyo. She could have been as easily cast as "Tokyo Rose" as had Iva Toguri. She had been called to testify three years before at Iva's trial in San Francisco, along with a large group of Japanese witnesses. After the trial, many of the group had been brought to New York to testify at my grand jury hearing. Ruth Hayakawa would later describe the trip as a sightseeing excursion, a "Sunday picnic".

There was an odd connection between two of my lawyers and two of the prosecution's witnesses. Both Murray Gottesman and George Plotkin had worked for the U.S. Judge Advocate at the War Crimes trials in postwar Tokyo. Sergeant Seitaro Fukita had been defended by Murray Gottesman and had been convicted of executing Captain Thomson. Another prosecution witness, USAF Captain Sakakida, had also been a prosecution witness at Fujita's trial. Plotkin and Gottesman knew a great deal more about Sakakida's wartime experiences than they could use in court.

On the first day of the trial, the jury was picked and the defense made motions for dismissal on several issues. First, the Army had held me without charges and without counsel for eight months after the war, had completely investigated my entire case while the memories of those involved were still fresh. I had been cleared of suspicion and given an honorable discharge and this present trial constituted double jeopardy. Motion denied.

Second, I had been held without charges and without counsel on numerous occasions during my second period of enlistment in the Army. Motion denied.

Third, that the court had no jurisdiction since the alleged

events had taken place in the Pacific. Motion denied.

On October 28, the second day of the trial, the prosecution and defense teams made their opening statements. Prosecutor Moses Kove portrayed me as a "perfidious traitor" who had been sympathetic to the Japanese cause, had helped mistreat my fellow prisoners and was indirectly responsible for the death of an American captain who had refused to do the Japanese bidding; that I went to the Japanese and said that I spoke the language, was a Buddhist and had offered my services; that I shaved my head, wore Japanese garb and had enjoyed freedom of movement within a few days of capture; that in a fit of anger I had reported Captain Thomson, who was taken out and shot by a Japanese sergeant and an enlisted man.

Murray Gottesman and George Plotkin painted me in a much different light. They described me as a sincere young man who had been a devotee of Buddhism from an early age, that I had spent a year in a monastic school in Japan, that I was a soldier who professed my love for my country night after night, who believed my country would be victorious and said so; that I was pressed into service as an interpreter; that I was driven into erratic, but not traitorous behavior by the privations of prison camp, and had only done what my superiors had told me to do. Above all, the defense would prove that the charge of being responsible for Captain Thomson's death was absolutely unfounded. The defense would show that Major Cousens and Captain Ince had issued orders to broadcast and that they would appear as witnesses.

The prosecution's portion of the trial was twenty days of testimony during which I sat dumbfounded as I listened to people I had met briefly on Corregidor and who recounted ugly, distorted and embellished accounts of what had happened there. It was only the fact that they kept using my name that I could keep in mind that they were testifying about me. My behavior had been unprecedented, and perhaps even bizarre, of that I was well aware: but the portrait drawn by the prosecution caricaturized me as treacherous, evil, and even fiendish.

The case against me had been pending during the entirety of Irving Saypol's tenure as U.S. Attorney. In January of 1952, he had been inducted as a justice in the New York State Supreme Court. He had won many important convictions as a federal prosecutor including the Rosenbergs'. Now, in the middle of November 1952 he was still involved in bringing my trial to a conclusion, and at the same time, having troubles of his own. A man named Armand Chankalian had been chief clerk and administrative assistant in the U.S. Attorney's office, Southern District of New York for fourteen years. On November 14, Chankalian testified before a State Crime Commission hearing that a number of high government officials including Judge Saypol, had had social contacts with, and dined with underworld chief, Thomas Luchese also known as "Three Finger Brown".

Saypol was eager to end my trial, and asked the Plotkins to consider a plea bargain. The Plotkins replied that they wouldn't dare carry such an offer to me. Saypol would have to present it himself face-to-face.

I was taken down to the federal courthouse at Foley Square and ushered into Saypol's office. Saypol asked the U.S. Marshal who had escorted me in to leave the room, then offered me a cigar, which I accepted. Saypol began, "You know we've got the goods on you and we're going to burn you..." I broke in: "Mr. Saypol, I only consented to come down here to see you to tell you I am not guilty of any of these charges." Saypol flushed with anger and called the marshal back in. "Get him out of here, get him out of my sight! Gimme that cigar." and he snatched it from my hand.

The marshal led me back downstairs, but when we reached the holding cell, word came that Saypol had called down and ordered me to be brought back to his office. This time I didn't bother to sit down. Saypol made his proposal. "Come on now, why don't you be reasonable. Get the government off the hook. Just pick any count in the indictment, give us a statement of culpability in court, and we'll send you to the country club at Danbury. You'll be out in 18 months." I replied, "So now you're going to trade with the traitor. Well, you don't have my price, Mr. Saypol, and I'm going to take you all the way!" I was returned to West Street, and the trial resumed.

The prosecution had decided to abandon the attempt to convict me on all but two of the broadcast charges. When the prosecution abruptly ended its case on December 10, it had failed to provide the constitutionally required two witnesses to each alleged act of treason. However, the effect on me had been exhausting and emotionally devastating; and the effect on the jury was irreversible. The sheer number of prosecution witnesses, even though their testimony did not concern counts of the indictment on which I was convicted, created an overall tone that was impossible to erase from the jury's memory.

My mood was morose by December 10 and I had little

hope that the defense would be able to alter the course of the trial. The defense called one important witness before the proceedings were adjourned for the holidays: General Jonathan Wainwright. The prosecution had made a pronouncement early in the trial that General Wainwright would take the stand to corroborate the testimony of the star prosecution witness, but the general had refused. Instead, when the defense requested that he testify in my behalf, Wainwright managed to come from his sickbed in Texas to do so.

General Wainwright made an impressive witness, and he spoke of the horrible days on Corregidor and the years of prison camp, some of which he had spent at Karenko and Shirakawa at the same time as me. Nevertheless, the only statements that he could truthfully make about my case was that he had not witnessed or heard of any act of treason on my part during that entire time. It was not exactly testimony that could refute the specific allegations of the indictment. Wainwright did testify that he and other Generals had been forced to do menial labor by the Japanese, and that they had even been forced to write commentaries and to make some broadcasts. Again his testimony did little to tear into the heart of the government's case. His appearance had been a great boost to my morale, but of little real help.

During the holiday adjournment, Gottesman was dispatched to the Far East to get depositions from Japan and Australia, but year's end delays in Japan prevented him from completing the most important part of his mission; going to Australia to get Major Cousens' statement, which was vital to my defense against the broadcast charges.

Wallace Ince, still on active duty with the Army, had been

transferred out of the country and therefore inaccessible to subpoena: There would be virtually no defense to the charges of broadcasting for the Japanese except my own testimony.

When the trial resumed, the defense team produced a number of witnesses that had known me well on Corregidor and during the years of prison camp on Taiwan. They were people who had been close to me and to the events that had been so grossly misinterpreted. They all testified to my loyalty, my efforts to make life better for my fellow prisoners, and that I had had as much apprehension about falling into enemy hands as any of them.

My friend Ray Makepeace testified that I was a patriot, and that I would have preferred that the besieged garrison fight to the death rather than surrender.

Navy Lieutenant Sam Bowler, when called as a prosecution witness, had been extremely careful in his testimony not to allow his words to be distorted to fit the government's scenario. Lt. Bowler returned to the stand as a defense witness to add that I had been "...in all respects, very much a perfect gentleman," and to make sure that it was understood that I had never received any kind of favor or preferred treatment for any of the interpreting I had done between the Japanese and Allied personnel.

A former Army physician, Colonel Braddock testified that I had often risked getting beaten up by interceding on behalf of other prisoners.

Several witnesses came to the stand to testify to my constant attempts to ease conditions for all prisoners, and that I hadn't been rewarded by the Japanese for anything that I did.

George Dixon testified to a specific incident when he had been brutally beaten by the Japanese and that I had interceded and was able to get them to stop.

Colonel Menzies and his wife, Mary Bernice Menzies, both appeared in my defense. They had been married about a month before the surrender in Malinta Tunnel. He had been my immediate superior and she had been a nurse in Malinta Hospital. They both testified that I had saved the Colonel's life and that I had been able to prevent a rape in the nurse's quarters. They had been close to me in the days after the surrender, they had both been in Malinta hospital at the time when most of the incidents were suppose to have happened, and they would have certainly known about it if I had been working for the Japanese.

Dr. Heimbach testified that he had known me well in Malinta Tunnel and the hospital and that he knew that I had been the object of many suspicions, and that he had also known for a fact that they were unfounded. Dr. Heimbach had been the one that had found me near death from another doctor's murder attempt, and had revived me. He testified obliquely to that fact by saying that many Allied personnel would have killed him if they had gotten the chance. Both Heimbach and I knew that the would-be murderer had testified for the prosecution.

Dr. Heimbach testified that I had walked with "a curious dignity and floating steps" and that it had exacerbated the suspicions about me. Indeed, I had been experiencing a much different level of awareness than those around me, "living in another world." Even those closest to me and who knew the indictment to be false could have truthfully testified that I was not quite in touch with reality: I would have to agree with that; I was not absorbed in their reality, I had access to a perfect world that existed within their hell. I was out of touch, at times, with the everyday reality, but not insane.

In the entirety of the defense's efforts, there was no attempt made to directly oppose the government's allegations or to say that they were false and completely fabricated. The only one who could testify to that directly was myself.

I took the stand to testify in my own behalf, vehemently denying all the government's charges. I testified that it had been my intent through the entire term of captivity on Corregidor to aid all the captured personnel using whatever devices available to me to improve conditions for them.

The defense placed into evidence documents that demonstrated that the Army, after making a lengthy investigation immediately at the end of the war, had cleared me of all charges, had given me an honorable discharge, allowed me to re-enlist, and had even recommended me to Officer's Candidate School.

The prosecution in cross examination attempted to get me to acknowledge a statement that I had signed during one of the innumerable interrogations conducted by a variety of government agents during the course of my lengthy incarceration. I insisted that I couldn't have known what the statement said and still have signed it. I had signed it without reading it.

Finally, in an attempt to complete the unsavory portrait of me in the eyes of the jury, Saypol revealed that I had been charged with an alleged homosexual act during my second Army enlistment.

The jury returned a verdict of guilty on four counts: 1) that I had offered my services to the Japanese, 2) that I had contributed to the death of Captain Thomson, and 3) and 4) that I had participated in two propaganda broadcasts.

Even after they had found me guilty of treason, I remarked that if I had been on that jury, and had to decide on the testimony presented them, that I would have voted guilty as well. I could understand how the jury had been led to this erroneous conclusion, but the prosecution had failed to fulfill the constitutional requisites for a conviction of treason, that there be two witnesses to an overt act of treason, or that the defendant make an admission of guilt in open court.

Two witnesses to an overt act of offering my services to the Japanese would both have had to be present at the same time and would both have to understand the Japanese language. The witness who had been produced to corroborate the testimony of the prosecution's star witness could not. He could only testify that I had said something in Japanese. The star witness himself, Air Force Intelligence Captain Richard Sakakida, had been captured on Corregidor and had spent the war years in the Philippines, and was forced to admit under Plotkin's cross examination that he had served as interpreter for a Japanese kangaroo court in Manila that resulted in the executions of five American officers. Had Sakakida been subjected to the same bias and suspicion that I had been, it would have been Sakakida on trial for his life. It was further established that he had served for nearly two years on the staff of General Yamashita, who was later hanged as a war criminal.

Two witnesses to the alleged overt act that was supposed to have contributed to Captain Thomson's death should have been produced. They were not. The prosecution did not even identify a specific alleged act nor demonstrate a causal relationship between it and the execution of Captain Thomson: Presumably, it was to have been something that I had said to a Japanese guard, and it would have had to have been made in Japanese. There would have to had been two Japanese-speaking witnesses both present at the scene and in the courtroom. There were not.

There were not two witnesses to my allegedly treasonous broadcasts. It must have seemed odd that in 18 months of participation in broadcasts with over 40 other Allied POW's, that there were only two which were "traitorous". The worse of the two was one made when the POW's had first arrived in Tokyo; one that I had been ordered to read over my objections. The portion quoted in the courtroom was that Pearl Harbor had occurred "...as a result of diplomatic blunders and pursuant of a selfish dictatorial foreign policy toward Japan."

Finally, the government failed to show that I had any intent to commit treason. Nevertheless, I was sentenced to life imprisonment by Judge Noonan, February 17, 1953.

I was returned to West Street where I was held for the next year and a half while my motions were considered simultaneously by Judge Noonan in District Court and by the U.S. Circuit Court of Appeals. The Appellate Court reversed my conviction on August 27, 1954.

The reversal was based on two strong points. First, that the prosecution had no right to bring up the issue of the homosexual charge: "...No authority has been cited that homosexuality indicates a propensity to disregard the obligation of an oath. The sole purpose and effect of this examination was to humiliate and degrade the defendant and increase the probability that he would be convicted, not for the crime charged, but for his general unsavory character. Permitting it was an error. The error was plainly prejudicial." The second point in the court's decision was that I had been arrested in Maryland at the point when the Army had decided not to press its own charges, but still held me in confinement at the Justice Department's request. The law reads that trial for an offense committed out of jurisdiction of any state or federal judicial district shall be conducted in the district where the offender is "found", meaning first apprehended, arrested or taken into custody under charges later found in the indictment. Therefore the District Court in New York had no jurisdiction. The prosecution had been its own undoing. Its own dirty tricks had been its weakness.

The successful appeal, however, did not set me free, since it did not rule on my guilt or innocence. My status was again one of a suspected traitor held without bail. A new grand jury was convened in Baltimore, Maryland, in the district of proper venue.

I learned a great deal about constitutional law in my five years at West Street and had studied every case of treason on the books. I wrote my own petition for a writ of habeas corpus and motions to dismiss the new indictment on grounds that I had been denied a speedy trial and that further prosecution would deny me my rights under the Fifth Amendment regarding the due process of law.

On November 25, 1954, I was taken to the District Court in Baltimore where I pleaded not guilty. I had felt renewed by the successful appeal in New York and I felt in retrospect that the experience would prove a valuable rehearsal. I was eager to confront the charges against me: It couldn't be any worse than New York and I sensed that the vigor had gone out of the government's resolve.

Since the Federal government had no detention facilities in Baltimore, I was taken to the City Jail. I spent about three months there.

Abruptly, on March 14, 1955, Judge Roszel Thompson set me free. In his 33-page decision, Judge Thompson granted my own motion to dismiss the entire case.

Judge Roszel C. Thompson was an honest and astute veteran of the Federal bench. From the very first hearing before Judge Thompson, I could sense that he seemed impatient with the Federal prosecutors and horrified about all the delays and manipulations that the Justice Department had employed in my case. On March 14th he had said almost in disgust to the prosecutors that he wanted this man released immediately and that he wouldn't entertain any objections. His decision described, in the section entitled "findings of fact", all the relevant details of my history; my adolescent interest in Buddhism, my monastic studies in Japan, an outline of my wartime movements, my incarceration after the war, my release, my honorable discharge, my re-enlistment, my various periods of confinement while in the Army. Then Judge Thompson recounted the details of the conspiracy to have me tried in New York. Quoting from a memorandum of a telephone conversation between Pentagon Liaison Officer Colonel Miller and Noel Story, an attorney with the Justice Department concerning my treason case:

"Mr. Story: I discussed the Provoo situation with Mr. Whearty and Mr. Foley. You people have to take some action; would it be possible for the Army to go ahead and take action under Section 8, and if the action is to the effect that Provoo will be released from the Army, would it be possible that he be discharged in New York so as to bring him within the jurisdiction of the (Southern) District Court?' The reason for this is that if we pick him up or arrest him in San Francisco, we have to take action within a very short time. We have a little more liberal set-up in New York. We can hold him for a longer time and finish the investigation before seeking an indictment. Is it possible to discharge Provoo in the (Southern) District of New York, at Governor's Island?"

"Colonel Miller: Do you have any idea where he entered the service?"

"Mr. Story: No, probably in San Francisco, his home. From our standpoint, San Francisco would have been a good place to have him discharged, but because of the fact that we will have to be ready to seek an indictment at the time he will be released, we will have difficulty in having him discharged in San Francisco.

"Colonel Miller: Do you plan to have the complaint ready at the time of his discharge, and then if you were in New York, would you have more leeway in getting indictment and holding him in the meantime?

"Mr. Story: You understand jurisdiction in treason cases, wherever a man is found, or if we bring him back from overseas, the point at which he entered the United States. We would have to work out an agreement when you get ready to release him; we will have someone there to arrest him and put him in custody.

"Colonel Miller: What is the jurisdiction if he is at Fort Meade?

"Mr. Story: We do not want that because it is an undesirable place for us to proceed in cases of treason. We do not get cooperation from the U.S. Attorney or the District Judge."

They had a more "cooperative" Judge and U.S. Attorney in that jurisdiction, and therefore they could hold me for a much longer time there without taking any action! Actually, the Judge that Mr. Story had in mind would not be sworn in for two more months, and the U.S. Attorney would not be promoted to that position until the same day. My case could be delayed that long, easily, so they could have their team in place

Judge Thompson remarked in his decision that "...Of course, it is not the function of a judge to 'cooperate' with either the government or the defendant in a criminal case." He went on to rule that among the many delays in his detailed account of the proceedings there came a point at which the defense was ready for trial and that the prosecution was solely responsible for delaying more than a year longer; he wrote that, "It therefore appears that a large part of the long delay, at least five years, has been due to the deliberate choice of the government, exercised for a supposed advantage."

I was freed in March, and in October the same year the U.S. Supreme Court affirmed the decision, in effect ruling that the government could not proceed against me in the matter again.

At last my freedom was complete, I thought. My inward and outward circumstances were unlimited. I reflected back on it all, and found that it was not quite over: I carried an enormous amount of emotional burdens, chains that draped my shoulders and led off behind me into my past. I was chained to the wreckage of thirteen years on a solitary reef. There would be many celebrations following my rescue, but when they were over I found I had left too much of myself behind.

Nichijo

Chapter Fourteen

Shipwreck

In thirteen years, the threat of execution had become such a routine part of my environment that it held no terror. Like one who had come to accept a terminal illness, I held no fear of it. Like the drone of an ocean liner's engines, constant during a long crossing, reminders of my jeopardy had become unnoticeable background.

Now that threat had become noticeable because it had suddenly stopped. The end of my official persecution made me realize again what enormous pressure I had been under and how much my responses had been suppressed. My release warranted a celebration, of course, and there were many dinners and parties to congratulate me and honor my attorneys. Finally the parties were over and sobriety returned and what lay before me was the task of finding my way through "real life".

The postwar years in the Army had presented their own form of hell, insinuations, rumors, harassment, oblique charges and investigations without conclusion. The years awaiting trail and the trials themselves had been an improvement in one important sense: the government had had to make its charges in the open, where they could be dealt with; challenged, confronted, countered, disproved. In the years following my trials, persecution was slow in fading away, and it had taken on some new forms. In particular it was the curse of having been convicted in the press and thereby in the public memory. Such media myths do not include the reversal of their condemnation. There had been small items in the newspapers announcing the reversal of my conviction, the dismissal of the second trial, and the subsequent Supreme Court decision. In comparison to the sensational fanfare that had announced the government's fable, and the dramatic headlines that had crowned me "Tokyo John" and "The Traitor of Corregidor", my exit from the public's attention had been inaudible. I hadn't been victorious, I hadn't won acquittal; I had merely maneuvered the government to a stalemate. In the public eye, I had gotten off on a technicality. In my own mind, I had deserved to win an acquittal: it was the government that had gotten off on a technicality.

I had been corresponding with a girl from Pennsylvania while I was imprisoned and she came down to Baltimore to meet me and to help me celebrate. In a short while, we were married, and returned to her hometown. I held several jobs for a short while as a carpenter, a gas station attendant and as an orderly at St. Mary's Hospital. I finally found work at the Spear Carbon Works. I had been completely honest about my legal history when I applied for work, and the management was willing to accept it. The company held several government contracts, however, some of them having to do with nuclear weapons, and management got the word that they would have to let me go. There would continue to be semi-official harassment.

The government continued to be an impediment to my

rehabilitation in a more direct way as well. I reopened the matter of my VA benefits and unpaid bonuses but received only terse bureaucratic replies, citing regulations that deny VA benefits to persons convicted of treason. In spite of the reversal of the conviction and the dismissal of the new indictment, portions of the government continued to act officially on the thesis that I had been guilty, and had escaped on a technical issue. The Veteran's Administration seemed to make its own interpretation of Supreme Court pronouncements.

In the minds of many people, armchair jurors in the media trial, I was guilty but had escaped official punishment on a fluke. My name and picture had been so much before the public that I was often recognized in the streets, and even more often when I was introduced by name. I never knew what to expect when I was recognized; sometimes it was, "Gee, I'm glad to meet you... it sure was a raw deal you got there..."; sometimes it was, "It's you, you lousy traitor!"; and more than once I was physically attacked.

The ten years following my release from legal jeopardy was an unhappy odyssey, which I would come to describe as dragging an enormous shipwreck of a reputation through the hostile swamps the government and the media had created for me. It was like the period of postwar Army enlistment in which a dossier of suspicions had followed me from camp to camp, interfering with all of my associations. It was something there was no way of confronting; there was no arena in which to take on my accusers; there was no forum in which to clear the air.

My employment was often foreshortened by the discovery

of my reputation or by the direction of my unseen persecutors, and if I did anything that was noteworthy enough to be mentioned in the papers, some reporter would research my past and write a follow-up article that would renew the entire affair. I increasingly confined my activities to working among the poor, the underprivileged and the sick: doing social welfare work with the Salvation Army and supporting myself working at hospitals.

From time to time I would be asked to give a talk on Buddhism, which boosted my spirits temporarily, and it reminded me of the higher calling I had once chosen and the paradise I had enjoyed at Minobu. I had gotten sidetracked...a horrible war, years of imprisonment, an exile within the military, long years a political prisoner, and now, social exile within the civilian population. I didn't want to drag my shipwreck back to Minobu. In a sense, I had begun to believe the government's portrait of my character ...I felt unworthy of Minobu.

My second wife had been unable to deal with it all, and I could hardly blame her. We divorced. My third wife had fared little better. We had moved to Virginia where I had family ties, but she was unhappy there far from her friends and her own family, and we divorced as well.

It was the winter of 1964, and I was unable to keep up the payments on our car by myself, so I let it go. I had no money and worse, I had no inspiration. I just left one day heading north. I had enough bus fare to make it to Washington, D.C., and that's all. I stayed overnight in a gospel mission there, and the next day hitchhiked north to Baltimore, where I had found work before. I checked the situation at all the hospitals with no luck. I spent the night in a rescue mission again. The next day I continued hitchhiking north into Pennsylvania. I was dropped off near the town of Williamsport and began walking, I didn't know where to. It was snowing and my clothes were inadequate for the cold and my shipwreck seemed especially burdensome. I was walking along the road in the snow reviewing all the times someone had been trying to kill me and I began entertaining the idea that it would have been just as well if I had allowed it to happen ...if I had been killed long ago. If a bomb had fallen on me running across the smoldering moonscape of Corregidor, if I had been judged a spy by the Japanese tribunal and shot down like Captain Thomson; if I had been beheaded for offering ice water to a Japanese field marshal; if I had succumbed to the injection given me in Malinta Hospital; if I had died of beri-beri at Karenko; if American bombs had fallen on Radio Tokyo; if I had burned in the electric chair at Sing-Sing like the Rosenbergs. Finally, there was no other motive to put one foot in front of the other, and I stopped. I moved myself a short distance off the road and lay down in the snow. Snow fell lightly on my face and began to cover me and I just let myself go.

A family that lived nearby found me several hours later. They had seen my shoulder sticking out of a mound of snow by the roadside. I was stiff and nearly dead. I awoke in a warm bed piled high with blankets and hot water bottles. I was in the home of a family of devout Christians more than willing to nurse a helpless stranger back to health. I remembered the icy heart with which I had resolved to die, but I could not prevent it from thawing in the warm bed of their unselfishness. I had truly been reborn.

They encouraged me to stay as long as I needed to regain

my strength, both physical and spiritual. Their love was all that I had needed. Like all of my darkest moments, help had appeared from an unexpected source. I had reached the bottom, the very bottom, and it had found me there, too. I found a job at the Polyclinic Hospital in Williamsport, sometimes working in the emergency room and on ambulance runs, and life was slowly rebuilt in the material sense; my inner strength had been totally renewed by the family of good Samaritans. One day in a Japanese grocery store where I had gone to pick up some of my favorite foods, I was introduced to Ralph Lindquist. He was a successful young insurance salesman who was an ardent enthusiast of karate.

While he was in the military forces in Korea he had become interested in Buddhism. On an R & R leave in Japan he had entered a Zen temple. No one there could speak English and he could speak no Japanese, but he had been able to go along with the routine and fit himself in. He meditated a great deal and had some dramatic flashes of insight. When he had returned to the U. S. and had taken up residence on the east coast, he had been unable to locate any English speaking Buddhist priests or teachers until he had run across me. The first time we met we talked for at least ten hours without stopping.

Ralph had formed a karate dojo (place of training) and wanted me to come and teach conversational Japanese to his members. Several members became interested in Buddhism and I began to hold classes in that, too. The questions of the students teach the teacher, and in answering them, I reviewed for myself all I had ever known about Buddhism.

It had been over twenty years since I left Minobu, and the

leaves ...Reflecting on these conditions of my present life, I often think, so must it have been with Buddha, when he was in search of truth and disciplining himself in expiation and mortification...

"Having served the masters,

By collecting wood and gathering herbs,

And by fetching water for them,

I have at last attained this enlightenment-

The enlightenment in the Lotus of Truth"

---from Nichiren, the Buddhist Prophet, Masaharu Anesaki, 1916.

The events of reality are never as simple as they are in our myths, and I was not here to spend my final days in sublime repose; I was here to receive training, to perfect my understanding of the Lotus, and to continue the mission to spread the teaching throughout the world. As I had learned from the British officers on Taiwan, "duty is a thing never done", and my duty now was solely to the Lotus.

I was raised in rank to Sozu (Right Reverend) so that I would be eligible for advanced trainings. I was at first housed in the dormitory until my own quarters could be built for me. I entered the shugyo training, a strenuous ascetic practice; arising before dawn, a cold water bath, a lengthy service chanting the sutra, before joining the procession to the morning otsutome. Each morning after the otsutome, I would go to the Lord Abbot's villa. Every two or three days the Abbot would say, "is there something you wish to ask?" and I would offer my interpretation of a particular point and ask if it was correct. I also began to ask if I might be included in a very high training, the "Arai Gyodo"--the "One Hundred Days in Winter", an ordeal of cleansing and purification. The Lord Abbot would put me off.

I had easily entered into the life of the monastery. The regimen that had been difficult and harsh to me as a young novice was now easy. I didn't have the pressure of being in a strange country that was preparing for war against my own, and the students in my English classes at Minobusan College were not sickly and green from malnutrition.

I made many excursions to the various shrines in Japan commemorating the events of Nichiren's life. To his birthplace at Kominato, where he entered a monastery at the age of eleven, and had been saved by a flash of light from his ojuzu beads; to Kamakura where the white monkey had led him away from a mob's murderous plot, and the spot where the executioner had been bedazzled by a comet; to his place' of exile on Sado Island; and returning, of course, to the most important shrine of all, Nichiren's tomb at his sylvan retreat, Minobu.

Finally, the Lord Abbot informed me that I would be allowed to participate in the Arai Gyodo--beginning in the middle of November. There had been snow on the ground for several weeks and the crisp mountain air cut through our usual robes, but the clothing for the Arai Gyodo was to be a single cotton garment, and no shoes at all. The regular meals at Minobu had been Spartan, but for the monks of the Arai

Gyodo, there would be a cup of rice and soup once a day, and a cup of tea at another time. I believed that I could survive on this ration for three months: I had lived for years on less.

There is a big difference, however, in what one must endure and what one chooses to endure. Imposed discipline is easier in a way than self discipline; and those participating in the Arai Gyodo could leave whenever they wanted, though it would mean they would have to leave Minobu in disgrace.

Many old monks were taking part this time, some of whom had taken the purification as many as fifteen times before. At least four masters participated in order to conduct the training.

The day begins with a pre-dawn ice water bath, and the chanting begins, as the monks walk around and around in a circle, barefoot in the snow. Each hour we stop for an ice water bath, then return to our chanting and their circular procession in the snow. Twenty-one ice water baths a day, three hours sleep, one hundred days; this is the Arai Gyodo, a "purification place", "One Hundred Days in Winter."

In a few days I felt like I wasn't going to make it. It was much more difficult than I had anticipated. Food, warmth and sleep were just outside the temple gate. Our feet became cracked and bloody, and our path, a red circle in the white snow. There was a vat of warm sake from which we could drink whenever we wanted, but the old timers cautioned me to avoid it. Likewise there was a choice of a warm bath every two weeks, but the old ones told me I would be better off without that as well.

We chanted "Namu Myoho-renge-kyo", "Adoration to

the Lotus, to the mysterious perfection of everything, just as it is." The sound of our voices became hoarse and cracked and the source of the tones moved to deep inside, so that the chanting took on a guttural resonation. The voices from stomachs became a communal heartbeat fusing our bodies and spirits into one. I began to experience my body disappearing, or rather, revealing its etheric true nature, an illusion as insubstantial as my own individual identity, my "self": a puppet's fantasy. My being became centered and calm ...and "here". I knew that I would make it.

The others had reached this plane as well, and our combined states of mind and our constant chanting was creating a spiritual vortex. The energy of each monk in the circle seemed combined with the rest, the group becoming one being, the individuals as the fingers of one hand, one mind.

After three-quarters of the hundred days had elapsed, I had reached the state of mind that I wanted this to go on forever, and I could understand why the old ones had come again and again. One old monk died during the ritual, and I could see what a sublime death it was, and we were certain that the old monk had been happy to have ended that way.

Having been prepared in this manner, the participants were ready to receive the highest teachings of the order. The attendant masters delivered occult training in the healing arts based on the 16th Chapter of the Lotus Sutra. The teachings of the Arai Gyodo are secret and are not described to outsiders.

Finally, the Hundred Days in Winter have passed and it is over; but for the others, and myself it is too soon. How to leave such a state? It is customarily arranged that some strong supporter of the priest's teaching is there to greet him as he emerges. For me, it was Ralph Lindquist, the man with the Karate Dojo in Pennsylvania, who had been instrumental in my return to teaching Buddhism.

Shortly after completing the Arai Gyodo, I was raised in rank to something on the order of Bishop, with the authority to ordain priests. I was given the name Nichijo Shaka. Nichijo means "sun-vehicle", and Shaka is the Japanese spelling of the name of the clan from which emerged the original historic Buddha, the Sakya clan.

Following my ordination ceremony, I walked down to the village of Minobu's outer gate, to make the traditional procession up through the winding main street of Minobu chanting "Namu Myoho-renge-kyo".

I was known to everyone in the village, and today, wearing my new insignia of high rank, I was honored and congratulated by all. The proprietors of every shop and inn asked me to stop and chant a sutra before each of their shrines. It was a triumphant procession, Minobu's version of a ticker tape parade. After some hours, I reached the huge Sammon Gate, entrance to the temple grounds, and retired to my quarters.

My first official function with my new rank came a few days later, when late one cold evening a schoolboy came to my quarters. The boy had come all the way up the dark stairs and through the monastery grounds to find me. There was an emergency in an old woman's home down by the river in the poorest part of the village. The woman wanted the "blue-eyed priest and no other".

I got robed, banked the ashes over the coals in my hibachi

to keep them going until I returned, and gathered my sutras and my cape. Guided by the schoolboy, we made our way down the mountain to the old woman's hut. The dilapidated thatched building was in an advanced state of disrepair. The old woman greeted me at the door and invited me to enter. She was bent way over from age and wore an old padded robe that was faded and had the stuffing coming out in several places. The straw mats on the floor were unraveling and her feet were bare; she hadn't even tabi. In her hibachi there were only a few small lumps of charcoal and it wasn't enough to keep the cottage warm, not with the holes in the walls.

Her tragedy was that her hibari bird was dead in its cage. It had died from the cold. She wanted the Lotus Sutra chanted for the happy transfiguration of her dead bird's spirit. I was touched by this and agreed.

Her shrine was clean, there were artificial flowers and a glass of water as an offering, and there was incense there for me to light. I took off my cape and began the service. I opened my sutra and chanted at least five chapters, the long version of the ceremony.

When it was over, the woman seemed much moved and had become very peaceful. She tried to make tea, but with her small amount of charcoal she could only make the water lukewarm, and the tea was weak when she served it.

She rummaged around in her belongings and found two 100-yen notes, wrinkled and dirty. They were worth about six cents. She didn't have the proper envelope, so she wrapped the notes in white paper and knelt down to offer them to me. It was the hardest danna I would ever have to accept. Danna is a Sanskrit term denoting that offering given to a priest which bears the connotation "...where it is understood that there is neither gift, giver or recipient." To have refused to accept it from the old woman would have been unthinkable, it would have been a cruel insult.

I returned to my quarters in the monastery. In the following days I arranged, in an indirect way, to have charcoal sent to the old woman's house as well as some nonperishable foodstuffs.

One of my students from Minobu College, Osamu Narita, had begun to petition me to accept him as my deshi, my student in Buddhist matters: At first I refused. I hadn't anticipated ordaining anyone until I returned to America. Also, it would be a break with tradition; no Caucasian had ever ordained a Japanese National in Japan. Young Narita was persistent and often brought me flowers and repeatedly asked to be accepted. One day when Narita had come to my quarters and been refused, Narita said to me, "Master, don't you know me?" At those words I had experienced satori, an instant flash of illumination. After that it was difficult to refuse. I asked the boy's father, and then discussed the matter with the Lord Abbot. Narita was shortly thereafter raised to full priest.

I had been trying to arrange a program for foreign students to be established at Minobu, and though I had the support of the Lord Abbot, I was meeting some resistance from the administrative hierarchy. A few days before my departure for America, I went to meet with the order's leaders at Shumuin headquarters in Tokyo. When they repeated their reluctance I confronted them head on and harangued them for their provincial attitude. I said that when I had established a temple in America, I would open the gates wide to all who wished to study the Lotus; Chinese, Koreans, Caucasians, anyone ...Nichiren was a saint for the world, not just Japan.

As I prepared myself for returning to America, I had several audiences with the Lord Abbot concerning establishment of the temple in America. How would the temple survive, how would I know where to build it, how would I raise the funds? The Lord Abbot answered, "If your teaching is valid, everything will support you, if it is not, nothing will."

Unlike before, leaving Japan this time had meaning and mission. Much had been resolved inwardly and outwardly during my training. I felt that the very nature of reality almost by conscious design, had guided me through the worst ordeals of life to reveal the innate symmetry of karmic justice: That whenever I had abandoned my fate, something unexpected had come to my rescue; that each time I was placed in captivity, among my captors there had been an ally; that within every destructive thing lies the seeds of its own destruction; that the machinations and maneuvers of my legal defense had not been able to prevent my conviction, it was the ruthlessness and dirty tricks of the prosecution that had ultimately freed me; that within a seemingly omnipotent government, dispassionately bent on my execution, there were men of justice. The perfect void within which all visible things exist acts as a mirror that reflects hatred and evil back on themselves; and love, giving and compassion back on themselves, too. Hatred need not be reciprocated, it is self-destructive; and love need not be rewarded, the giving of it is the source of happiness.

Chapter Sixteen

Puna

Coming back to America from the beauty of timeless Minobu, it seemed to me that nothing had happened in the intervening years. It was as though I was returning from my first learning experience at the great monastic center years before; as if the horrors of war, the long starvation and brutality of POW days, and the sordid aftermath through several court trials were as dreams. I was returning to San Francisco, or so I thought, to where everything had begun for me. How little life resembles our plans! It was not to be.

Arriving in Honolulu aboard a British cruise liner on a Sunday, I left the ship to visit the principal Nichiren Buddhist Temple. The chief priest was an old friend from pre-war days, formerly teaching in Seattle, Washington. It was a very pleasant reunion. He spoke English well and we talked for hours about all that had befallen us since our last meeting. When I told him I was en route to San Francisco and only to be in Hawaii for a few hours on a brief layover, he seemed both surprised and disappointed. The Bishop told me that I was needed in the islands, and I experienced a strange, fateful feeling: that this clicked suddenly as somehow right, though I knew I was expected on the mainland. I had left home originally in 1941 for the Far East and now it seemed I was returning at last to commence my mission, for which I had been so long in training; to try and serve as an interpreter of the wisdom of the East to my own people. I felt really free for the first time since 1941, and now it was 1967.

My first weeks of residence in Hawaii were spent at the Nichiren Temple in Honolulu. My predecessor in Hawaii, Reverend Ernest Shinkaku Hunt, had passed away in his 90's. My first trip out of the temple precincts was to chant the Lotus Sutra where Reverent Hunt's ashes were interred. Like many of us from the West, he had spent many years in the study and practice of different schools of the Mahayana: Hongwanji, True Pure Land School, and Zen.

I had previously visited Reverend Hunt in Hawaii in the 1930's, and I was struck again by the lush fragrant beauty of the flowers and the blossoming trees. Everywhere there was color. The sun and refreshing rain were daily miracles. Best of all, there was a climate of peace and aloha. Getting acquainted at the University of Hawaii, where I was asked to lecture, it was apparent that here was a rare atmosphere of true inquiry, learning and reciprocity. It was the long dreamed of openness, understanding, great vitality and awareness in a beautiful free setting, where mutual respect and interest flourished. How soul filling and delightful! It was in these first few months, here at last home and free, that long enduring friendships were formed. There I met Professor Richard Peterson, who has been my supporter and advisor in all things ever since.

The culmination of my life came about after moving my

seat (the temple) to the sparsely populated Puna District of the "Big Island" of Hawaii. Not the Hawaii of towering condominiums, honky-tonk metropolis and tour buses on the freeway; but Hawaii of the rusted tin roofs, mongoose on a rubbish heap and dirt road through a cane-field. I established my residence in a simple hermitage in the rain forest on the slopes of Kilauea volcano. When I die, it may be necessary to build a proper temple here, but today I live and I am the temple. When I had asked the Lord Abbot of Minobu about building a temple in America, and the Abbot had answered, "If you succeed, you have failed: when you succeed, you will be old ashes, to be discarded."

There in Puna, Professor Peterson and I found a small, very suitable acreage in a heavily forested area. It was serene and beautiful and located about 3 miles from the nearest village on a dead-end road; an ideal location for a spiritual retreat and training center. Here, in this beautiful quiet setting, I continued my meditation and expiation of those sins accumulated from all eternity. People came for retreats, to share the simple fare, work about our rustic shacks and discuss truths and the nature of reality. A profound peace settled on my heart, and I felt as if I were living in the very vestibule of paradise.

Still, something vaguely indefinable was lacking. As I reviewed the years of persecution, calumny, confinements and trials that together with my numerous hospitalizations resulting from stress and alcoholism, with declining health and the approaching shade of disintegration; it occurred to me that with my death, some part of the universal truth would be forever lost to the knowledge of man. I felt a commission to set down my memories before the hand of time erased them forever. A friend gave me a small tape recorder, and I began my narrative. It ran to over fifteen hours and took almost three months to complete. I had absolutely no records before me and had to rely on my still, except for recent events, excellent memory. I had known for years that I was mentally affected, but in no way impaired in my inner freedom and integrity.

Having dictated my life account in solitude and seclusion, for once without a gun at my back or a sword at my throat, it felt as if a large walk-in safe was lifted off my back. In the peace and purity of this forested retreat, surrounded by great trees, blossoms and fruit, an inner door opened, and I was filled with a deep sense of renewal. The best was yet to come. For years, I had been burdened with feelings of guilt, rage and resentment. Now a major change was taking place within me. Everything began to fit. I was increasingly aware of that vast area above and beyond self-centeredness: When I was young, and for marked periods thereafter, this consciousness had been my usual state. Now it was returning, and in greater depth. How marvelous that change, the constantly evolving process of life, never ceases! We go towards the light. "The Kingdom of God is spread upon the earth, and men do not see it." The idea took on new depth and imminent meaning. As tears of anguish bring clearer sight, so do years of justice denied bring glorious vision and some glimmer of knowingness. Life is the real trial, and without this insubstantial phantasmagoria of phenomenal existence, there can be no Nirvana. The ceaseless burden of expiation, alienation and exile has been lightened. The forest is filled with birdsong, and the faded flowers thrown from my little shrine cabinet take root and flourish in abundance. I think continually of the wonderful people who have come to my forest retreat to share with me the loving care and friendship while learning of the Dharma teaching. Each one is to me a perfect Lotus of truth.

"All things work together for good" has become electrically real. The higher power, intelligence, grace, eternal-that-which-is by whatever term we might employ, recreated the entire spectrum of the universe in splendor and in peace. Clarity resulted from meditation, and I became aware of the beautiful cosmic creativity and spontaneous nature of existence: In all of this, everything happened just as it should, without any preordained plan or intention of my own. It was as if I had spent the major portion of my existence trying to bring life to an arid plot of wasteland, and at long last miraculously there appeared flourishing fields of grain. Now my entire being resonates with a gratitude beyond understanding or expression. Words fail.

All praise and adoration be to all things, such as they now are; ever were; and ever will be.

In love and reverence, Nichijo, September 1984

Nichijo

The Bishop's Birthday - 1984

What a twisted tale of torment. Nichijo was deeply scarred by the events we've just described here. Yet to spend time with him in all his various haunts around Hilo and Puna, when it wasn't about Buddhism, it was about laughter and the enjoyment of present company.

By August 6, 1984, his 67th birthday, we knew each other pretty well. I was giving him a ride to his birthday celebration at a restaurant in Hilo. I picked him up at his dojo behind Pahoa and we stopped at the Pahoa Cash and Carry for a half pint of brandy. By the time we reached Keaau 8 miles later, he required another half pint from Akiyama Store. And one more stop before we continued on to Hilo, the Hongwanji, across the street and a few doors down. "It's my birthday, and I must honor my parents!"

Hongwanji is a popular form of Buddhism and most of the Japanese people in the Hawaiian Islands are so affiliated, and many attend Sunday services. A Hongwanji has the same layout as a Christian church. There are pews with an aisle down the middle, an altar at the front, a lectern from which the priest would expound the topic of the week and a raised choir box on the right. Except for the substitution the Amida Buddha for Jesus; a Baptist, Presbyterian or Catholic would feel right at home.

He invited me to go in with him. I reached the doors first and started to open one when I stopped. "Nichijo, there's already some kind of service going on in there!" He nodded, reached into his robe and pulled out a string of ojuzu beads. He said some words in Japanese, and then placed the beads around my neck. "It's all right," he said, "*We* are Buddhist priests!" We entered, walked to the front and sat down in the first row. After a few minutes sitting in respectful silence, he got up, approached the altar, lit some incense and paid homage to his parents in Japanese. We soon left and were on our way to Hilo. I have never passed myself off as a Buddhist priest, or even a Buddhist, but I treasure the beads and the story of how I got them.

As in most of the arenas of his life, Nichijo had earned a broad spectrum of reputations in East Hawaii in the 1980's. Many of my friends had encountered him in a variety of venues, and most of them had an outrageous story to tell about this complex character. Some people had a distaste of him, for one reason or another. To those of us who spent any time with him; he was funny, emotional, entertaining, histrionic, mercurial, uproarious, flamboyant, sometimes drunk, theatrical, problematic and fearless. And as zany as he could be at times, he was a serious Buddhist scholar and priest. At a public event commemorating the bombings of Hiroshima and Nagasaki at the Hilo Civic Center, Nichijo was standing in full robes on the platform with other robed clerics and local dignitaries, it was he that delivered the lead-off invocation. Apparently, he was the highest-ranking Buddhist Bishop in the Hawaiian Islands. He could get the island Mayor on the phone. He could get the Governor on the phone. He could get somebody out of jail on just his say-so. And like I described earlier, he could get his way at the Social Security Office.

He was gay, of course. He had enjoyed relations with several serious girlfriends, including three marriages, but he made no secret that his preference was for men. "Gay as a tree full of owls!" he would say of himself. I don't quite understand the reference, but I quote it here faithfully, as his self-portrait.

We decided to skirt the gay issue in the telling of his story. In the decision of the Appellate Court, "...No authority has been cited that homosexuality indicates a propensity to disregard the obligation of an oath. The sole purpose and effect of this examination was to humiliate and degrade the defendant and increase the probability that he would be convicted, not for the crime charged, but for his general unsavory character." It was prosecution dirty tricks that tried to connect the facts of his sexual orientation with treasonous acts, and should never have been part of the trial and, hence, not part of the chapters we call "The Testimony of John Provoo". In a more enlightened time, it would not have mattered.

I am not an investigative reporter and I invite more professional researchers to fill in the gaps in this narrative. In 1984 I corroborated what I could with the resources of the Hilo Library and their New York Times archive on microfilm. I don't have answers to the questions we've raised. I can only relate what Nichijo believed: that from the time he was identified as gay while working undercover in Manila, it was an element of the matrix of suspicion surrounding him. In the early 1950's, the Hoover-McCarthy-Cohn cabal conducted an anti-gay witch hunt that was nearly the equal of their anti-communist "Red Scare" often conflating the two as enemies of the state. Blacklisting and purges of gays and communists from important positions both in government and public life were everyday news stories. That mindset was certainly part of the post-war Justice Department's prosecution of Nichijo and many others.

Concerning other mysteries, my theories would only be slightly more informed than anyone who had read this book. The full story of the POW broadcast program has not been told. The roles of Ince and Cousens; and their handlers Ikeda and Domoto, has not been told. Were Iva Toguri and John Provoo responsible for what occurred at Radio Tokyo? Of course not, but they were the only ones punished. Was there a conspiracy to obscure the true facts? Obviously, but I don't know the who, the what or the why.

I am just a scribe in this telling. I am following the blueprint left for me by this departed friend. I am a carpenter who picked up a hitchhiker one day in rural Hawaii. And as we drove around country roads in my old pickup truck, I listened to his stories, and I wrote them down. He wanted to make sure that the unique thread of history he had witnessed was not lost, and I promised to bring it to light after he was gone.

There's one last thing that Nichijo told me that I want to share, and then I'll just leave it at that. I'm not even sure it's a Buddhist idea. Perhaps some reader can enlighten me. In my studies, I had never heard it before. He said, "Life is allegorical; It's telling you a story."

John Oliver, October 2014

Nichijo

ABOUT THE AUTHOR:

John Oliver earned Bachelor degrees in Political Science and Religious Studies at the University of California, Santa Barbara in 1969. In the 1970's, he discovered his passion for homebuilding, and has spent most of his life as an artisan building contractor in California and Hawaii. In a chance encounter with Bishop Nichijo Shaka on the rural Big Island in 1983, he found a direct use for his liberal arts education. His collaboration with Rev. Shaka resulted in the biography, "Nichijo", copyrighted in 1986, but never published. In 2014, living in semi-retirement in Sonoma County, California, he finally found the time to complete the thoughtful rewrite that was begun nearly 30 years before. "Nichijo: The Testimony of John Provoo" was released in October of 2014.

www.ingramcontent.com/pod-product-compliance
Lightning Source LLC
Chambersburg PA
CBHW060918040426

42445CB00011B/674